SCOTTISH CLANS
AND FAMILY NAMES

Their Arms, Origins and Tartans

SCOTTISH CLAN AND FAMILY NAMES

Their Arms, Origins and Tartans

Roddy Martine

Foreword by Malcolm Innes of Edingight CVO
Lord Lyon King of Arms

Heraldic illustrations by Don Pottinger LVO MA DA
Islay Herald

John Bartholomew & Son Limited
Edinburgh

This book was designed and produced by
Strawberry Hill Press Limited, 24 Walpole Road,
Twickenham, Middlesex TW2 5SN

First published in 1987 by John Bartholomew & Son Limited,
Duncan Street, Edinburgh EH9 1TA, Scotland

Layout by Tim Higgins
Edited by Raymond Kaye
Tartan photography by David Webster, Creative Audio Visual Productions Limited
Typeset by Wyvern Typesetting Limited, Bristol
Originated, printed and bound by Springbourne Press Limited, Basildon, Essex

British Library Cataloguing in Publication Data

Martine, Roddy
  Scottish clan and family names:
  their arms, origins and tartans.
  1. Tartans
  I. Title
  929'.2'09411   DA880.H76
  ISBN 0-7028-0773-7

TITLE PAGE *Kilchurn Castle, Loch Awe; see also p. 69. Scottish Field (J. Watt)*

FRONT COVER PICTURES *Crests from left to right (bottom): Somerville, Lord Somerville;
Spalding of Ashintully; Spens of Lathalen.*
*Crests from left to right (top): S(c)haw of Rothiemurchus; Sinclair, now Earl of Caithness;
Skene of that Ilk*
Tartans: (left) Wallace Hunting; (right) Ross Ancient
Picture: MacDonnell of Glengarry by Sir Henry Raeburn; see also pp. 15 and 139.
National Galleries of Scotland

BACK COVER PICTURE *Eilean Donan Castle; see also p. 166. Scottish Field (Alden)*
Standard: The Scottish Royal Standard

To Don Pottinger, MA (Hons), DA
Islay Herald of Arms,
whose kindness, humour and great courage
his friends will never forget

AUTHOR'S ACKNOWLEDGMENTS

Thanks must be given for the help and advice of a number of persons involved in the preparation of this book. In particular, the author would like to thank the many chiefs of clans and the secretaries of clan and family societies who kindly provided information. Particular thanks are due to Harry Lindley of Messrs Kinlock Anderson Ltd, manufacurers of Highland Dress, who kindly supplied the tartan samples used for reproduction. The author would also like to thank Simon Green for his assistance in the photographing of certain of the clan and family castles.

PUBLISHER'S ACKNOWLEDGMENTS

We gratefully acknowledge the assistance of the publishers of the *Scottish Field* magazine for their permission to use the illustrations of the Standards of the Scottish chiefs. These designs were created for the flags flown in Princes Street, Edinburgh for the duration of the 1977 International Gathering of the Clans. Thanks are also due to Messrs John Bartholomew and Sons Ltd for their permission to use the illustrations from the Clans Map *Scotland of Old* and Kinloch Anderson Limited, Edinburgh for their generous assistance in loaning tartan cloth samples for photography and to the following who have loaned photographs and/or colour transparencies:

BBC Hulton Picture Library: 53 (right)
British Tourist Authority: 117
Camera Press: 124, 138
Jenny Carter: 84, 141, 156, 167
Clan Donald Centre, Isle of Skye: 134
David Cormack: 148
Dennis Hardley: 194, 198
Inverness Museum: 23 (right)
F.M. Duncan, Dundee: 126
Roddy Martine: 19, 55, 57, 58, 60-61, 91, 101 (above), 103, 105, 108, 111, 113, 121, 123, 128, 170, 181, 182, 185, 193 (2), 196, 200, 201, 204, 207
W.R. McDowall, Edinburgh: 164
National Galleries of Scotland, Edinburgh: 15, 83, 110, 137, 169, 191 (top)

National Portrait Gallery, London: 22 (2), 23 (left), 27, 94 (below)
National Trust of Scotland: 120
Popperfoto: 104
Queensferry Photographers, Edinburgh: 87
Antonia Reeve Photography: 157
Sonia Roberts, London: 37
The Royal Collection, Holyrood House, Edinburgh, by Kind Permission of Her Majesty the Queen: 33
Tom Scott, Edinburgh: 109 (below)
Scottish Field Magazine, Glasgow: 53 (left), 63, 67 (John Watt), 68-69 (John Watt), 70 (John Watt), 73, 90, 94 (below) (John Watt), 99 (John Watt), 106 (John Watt), 99 (John Watt), 106 (John Watt), 109 Above) (George B. Alden), 112, 118-19 (George B. Alden), 127 (George B. Alden), 136-37 (John Watt), 139 (John Watt), 145, 153 (George B. Alden), 158 (George B. Alden) 160 George B. Alden), 161 (John Watt), 162, 168 (George B. Alden), 179 (John Watt), 180 (John Watt), 191 (below) (George B. Alden)
Scottish National Portrait Gallery, Edinburgh: 56
Scottish Tourist Board, Edinburgh: 22 (above), 28, 30, 30-31, 71, 116, 172
Van Hallan, Isleworth: 174
David Ward, London: 98
Woodmansterne Limited, Watford: 131

CONTENTS

The Arms of Her Majesty's Lord Lyon King of Arms

FOREWORD

by Malcolm Innes of Edingight CVO
Lord Lyon King of Arms

RODDY MARTINE HAS ALWAYS BEEN keenly interested in matters relating to Scottish life and culture. He has written books on Scottish dancing, on the Royal Family and their association with Scotland and on Royal ceremonies in Scotland, and prepared the informative and popular souvenir of the International Gathering of the Clans in Edinburgh in 1981. It is, therefore, in keeping with these interests that he should have produced this most attractive work on the subject of the origin and history of the clans and families, their tartans and the Armorial Bearings of the Chiefs.

Malcolm Innes of Edingight, CVO, *Lord Lyon King of Arms in ceremonial dress*

Those of us who are familiar with the emigration from Scotland that resulted from the Depression of the 1930s, from postwar difficulties and from the high unemployment that persists in Scotland, perhaps find it difficult to appreciate that for 200 years between 1097 and 1296 the high road to Scotland was an attractive prospect for younger sons of English families and families of Continental origin. At the close of the eleventh century Scotland held a mixture of Celtic and pre-Celtic peoples, the Picts, the Britons, the Irish (Scots), and also the Anglo-Saxons and the Scandinavians. David I and his two grandsons invited a vigorous group of Normans, Bretons and Flemish to come and provide leadership and to fortify central royal authority in Scotland, and within a relatively short period strong lordships had been founded from the Cheviots in the south to the Moray Firth in the north. By 1296 five of the ancient Earldoms of Scotland were in the hands of families of Continental origin: Sutherland (descendants of the Flemish Freskin), Buchan (Comyn), Angus (Umphraville), Menteith (Stewart) and Carrick (Bruce). In the course of looking through the entries in this book it will be seen that a very large number of Scottish families originated from these Continental families. From the abdication of John Baliol in 1296 until James VI succeeded Elizabeth in right of the Crown of England in 1603 there was little opportunity for the English to settle in Scotland or for Scots to settle in England.

I am particularly pleased that it has been possible to include illustrations of the Arms of so many Chiefs. It is perhaps not as generally understood as it might be that Scottish heraldry has been very significantly influenced by the clan and family organization in Scotland and the system of differencing for determinate cadets (those whose relationship to the Chief is known and proved) and indeterminate cadets (those whose relationship to the Chief is not known) has resulted in heraldic writers in Europe acknowledging that Scots heraldry is probably the purest system that has evolved. One result of Scots heraldry having developed in accordance with the clan and family social system in Scotland is that it remained popular and never became the mere preserve of an upper class. The clan system in Scotland has resulted in Scotland being relatively free from class distinctions and class consciousness.

While all the constituent elements of the Chiefly Arms – shield, crest and supporters – are the property of the individual Chief, every clansman can share in the pride of the Chief by displaying the crest badge, which consists of the crest of the Chief within a strap and buckle and the Chief's motto. This may be worn as a bonnet badge by men and as a brooch by ladies, and in appropriate circumstances this may now appear on certain furnishings within the house of the loyal follower of the Chief. Ownership and the recording of the undifferenced Arms in Lyon Register is the legal indication of Chiefship in Scotland and as a result of many careful decisions in Lyon Court over the last 50 years many clans and families have been able to reorganize effectively under a newly determined Chief. During the last 40 years the Standing Council of Scottish Chiefs has grown from a relatively small body to one that now consists of about 120 members, and it is of considerable standing and influence at the present time.

The reproductions of the tartans are of a particularly high quality in this book and readers will be struck by the variety of pattern they display and their age. Some are of considerable antiquity, but the majority are probably of early to mid-nineteenth-century origin, and others are of much more recent origin. As certain families that have been disorganized for a very long period come together again and are organized effectively under a newly determined Chief, a tartan is frequently desired. Thus from time to time new tartans are, at the request of the Chief, placed on record in Lyon Court Books. As clans and families are institutions of influence and significance in the organization of social life today in Scotland and overseas, it is perfectly natural that matters concerning such institutions should continue to evolve and no surprise should be felt that tartans continue to be devised. The newly devised tartan of today is the tartan of antiquity of the future.

I am sure that those who read this book will find much to interest them and will also be encouraged to read further on the clan or family that is of particular interest to them.

INTRODUCTION

A COUNTRY SUCH AS SCOTLAND with a relatively small population is naturally peopled by families who not only claim distant nationalistic origins, but close kinship with each other. In the Scotland of old, lands and fortunes were allocated by successive monarchs to the great families of the south and to the great clans of the north. With the passage of time these families and clans have been broken up and many of their descendants scattered around the world, divorced from whence they came. And so it is not altogether surprising that the associations and accessories of kinship have taken on an ever more poignant significance for those whose names are recorded in the history of the land of their forefathers.

This book concerns the clans and families of Scotland; and because the subject matter relates directly to the personal ancestry of so many individuals, there is bound to be considerable disagreement about interpretation. Researching this book could almost have led to the conclusion that each successive generation has chosen to adapt or rewrite individual clan or family histories to suit the whims of the time. But learned sources in this century, in particular Sir Thomas Innes of Learney and Sir Iain Moncreiffe of that Ilk, have contributed immeasurably towards untangling the intriguing jungle of Scotland's genealogical heritage; and throughout, the office of the Lord Lyon King of Arms has maintained the role of wise adjudicator with the final voice of approbation.

Sir Thomas Innes of Learney was one of Scotland's most distinguished Lord Lyons and an outstanding historian. His book, *The Tartans of the Clans and Families of Scotland*, first published in 1938, along with Frank Adam's *The Clans, Septs and Regiments of the Scottish Highlands*, 1908, are still undoubtedly the finest works on tartan to date. There have been many other publications on the subject, some of considerable distinction, and understandably it might be considered presumptuous to pretend to improve on any of the research and observations that have brought twentieth-century credibility to the structure of the clan system, to the emergence of the powerful families of the land – and to some of the myths of tartan, which has come to be recognized as the identifiable clan and family apparel of Scotland, despite the fact that this notion was almost entirely a late Georgian and Victorian indulgence. It must be said, however, that much of the professional and amateur study that has made the contents of this book possible was undertaken by those whose enthusiasms were first fired by Frank Adam, Sir Thomas and Sir Iain and those of their generations who cared about and were intrigued by the traditions and cultural heritage of their country.

The Scotland of old comprised Scots, Picts and Norsemen in the north; Angles or Saxons, Normans and Strathclyde Britons in the south. So there are fundamental racial and cultural differences to contend with in Scotland as a whole, despite the process of inbreeding over the centuries. Put simplistically, however, the clan (which is the Gaelic for family) belonged to the Highlands; the civilized south was dominated by noble houses and families. It is important to appreciate this differentiation, especially as it is common practice in America to refer to all Scots as being members of clans.

This book encompasses the clans and families prominent in Scottish history. Sept names and those of their retainers are also listed. The extensive colour content of this publication includes not only the reproduction of tartan samples, but also photographs of clan and family castles and houses or associated territories. In addition, Islay Herald Don Pottinger has provided illustrations of clan and family arms, and of the personal banners of the clan chiefs of Scotland where they have been matriculated.

Tartan and the clan system

Tartan, beyond dispute, is of ancient creation. However, what we know about its origins is for the most part subject to the fantasy, whims and interpretation of the past two hundred years. It is what tartan has stood for in the past and represents for the future that concerns us in this study.

Tartan is universally accepted as the national dress of the Scot. It is a means of recognition both on a national and personal level. It is a symbol of great pride and is of great importance in Scotland's cultural identity. One conclusion to emerge in the compilation of this book is that tartan is still a remarkable decorative fabric with an enduring role to play, even without its traditional associations. High fashion in Europe and America has been eager to exploit its appeal regardless of Scottish clan and family connections.

However, to understand the unique clan and family significance that tartan has come to hold for the present-day Scot, it is necessary first to explore the ancient role of clanship, a feudal egalitarian structure to which the majority of Scots, with the integration of Highlander with Lowlander over the centuries, nowadays like to claim affiliation, and for which tartan has latterly been accepted as the equivalent of a clan or family uniform.

In simple terms, the clan system of old Scotland encompassed a tribal civilization which afforded both a continual threat to, as well as an

OPPOSITE *MacDonnell of Glengarry by Sir Henry Raeburn*

14

instrument of government for, a Scottish legislature based in the south-east of the northern territory of what is now the United Kingdom of Great Britain. To comprehend how this came to be so, it is necessary to appreciate the structure of Scotland as a kingdom.

Our early records come from the first Christian church in Scotland, founded at Whithorn by St Ninian in AD 397. When the Romans left Britain in the course of the fifth century, the tribes, both original inhabitants and newcomers, divided themselves into four kingdoms: the kingdom of Dalriada in Argyll, made up of Celtic Scots and including some Christians; Strathclyde, where the people were Britons (akin to the Welsh and Cornish); the Lowlands, inhabited by Angles or Saxons; and the north, inhabited by Picts. Towards the end of the eighth century, Norsemen began to occupy Orkney and Shetland and parts of the Hebrides. In 843, King Kenneth MacAlpine, through his father's marriage to a Pictish princess, united the Scots and the Picts, forming the kingdom of Alba, which became known as Scotia. At this time, Kenneth moved his court from Dunstaffnage and Dunadd in Argyll to Scone in Perthshire, which became his seat of government. When Malcolm III, called Canmore, seized the throne of Scotland from Macbeth two hundred years later, he chose to take his court to Dunfermline. It was at this stage that the nature of Scotland's government began to change. Malcolm's second wife, who had left England soon after the Norman Conquest, was the devout Queen Margaret, granddaughter of the English king Edmund Ironside. She brought the practices of the Roman church to the Scottish court causing the decline of the ancient Celtic church. Many resented her anglicizing influence over Malcolm, particularly when it seemed that feudalism was being introduced.

It was from this period onwards that many Norman families began to arrive in Scotland to seek their fortunes. Under the Celtic system, land belonged to the tribe; under feudalism, all land belonged to the king who could distribute it at will. A compromise was found, although not strictly recognized. Under it the Scottish king was something between a monarch and a chief. He was the Ard Righ: the High King over the Righ or provincial kings and thus exercised the function of an ultimate feudal superior. (It is possible that it was in the light of this High Kingship that in later centuries the Scottish crown came to be regarded as an imperial one.) Internal clan loyalties, however, remained to the chief alone, whose pedigree brought entitlement to that office, but who was considered within the clan as the equal of every clansman even though he was their leader and, as such, not to be challenged.

Burt's letters from a gentleman in the north of Scotland, published in 1745, include the following description:

The Highlanders are divided into tribes or clans, under chiefs or chieftains, and each clan is divided into branches from the main stock, who have chieftains over them. These are subdivided into smaller branches of fifty or sixty men, who deduce their origin from their particular chieftains, and rely on them as their more immediate protectors and defenders. The ordinary Highlanders esteem it the most sublime degree of virtue to love their chief and pay him blind obedience, although it be in opposition to the Government.

Next to this love of their chief is that of the particular branch of which they sprang, and, in a third degree, to those of the whole clan or name, whom they will assist, right or wrong, against those of any other tribe with which they are at variance. They likewise owe goodwill to such clans as they esteem to be their particular well-wishers. And, lastly, they have an adherence to one another as Highlanders in opposition to the people of the low country, whom they despise as inferior to them in courage, and believe they have a right to plunder them whenever it is in their power. This last arises from a tradition that the Lowlands in old time were the possession of their ancestors. The chief exercises an arbitrary authority over his vassals, determines all their differences and disputes that happen among them, and levies taxed upon extraordinary occasions, such as the marriage of a daughter, building a house, or some pretence for his support or the honour of his name; and if anyone should refuse to contribute to the best of his ability, he is sure of severe treatment, and, if he persists in his obstinacy, he would be cast out of his tribe by general consent. The power of the chief is not supported by interest, as they are landlords, but by consanguinity, as lineally descended from the old patriarchs or fathers of the families, for they hold the same authority when they have lost their estates, as may appear from several instances, and particularly that of one, Lord Lovat, who commands his clan though at the same time they maintain him, having nothing left of his own. On the other hand, the chief, even against the laws, is bound to protect his followers, as they are sometimes called, be they never so criminal. He is their leader in clan quarrels, must free the necessitous from their arrears of rent, and maintain such who by accidents are fallen to total decay. Some of the chiefs have not only personal dislikes and enmity to each other, but there are also hereditary feuds between clan and clan, which have been handed down from one generation to another for several ages. These quarrels descend to the meanest vassals, and thus, sometimes an innocent person suffers for crimes committed by his tribe, at a vast distance of time, before his being began.

Malcolm Canmore's youngest son King David I built great abbeys to civilize his kingdom, to pay tribute to his saintly mother and, above all, to consolidate his rule. What better means than to use the church as your listening posts throughout the realm? However, he and his successors failed to gain firm control over the remoter tribes of the Highlands who were in ascendancy and determined to maintain their independent clan structure. It was, therefore, in the eleventh and twelfth centuries that we see these early Highland clans developing into the independent units that would identify and distinguish their society in later centuries. Their problems were divorced from those of the south of Scotland; the threat to their security came not from England, but from the Viking raiders from Norway and Denmark with their longships who plundered the islands and coastline of the north-west. Iona, for example, was burned three times by such Norsemen, who destroyed Dumbarton Castle, and by the tenth century had gained

Stirling Castle; see also p. 200

control of Orkney, Shetland and the Western Isles, while the Danes held the north and east of England.

Historians accept that a distinct division existed between the Highlands and Lowlands of Scotland, but this fell considerably beyond the so-called Highland Line. As Sir Thomas Innes stated: 'It was by no accident that the Firth of Forth was called "The Scottish Sea" and that Northern Scots in early times referred to Fife and Lothian as distinct from "Caledonia". The distinction of race and customs, as well as social characteristics run in a diagonal line through the Ochils rather than through the Grampians, and includes Renfrew and Galloway, both distinctly "Highland" compared with Lothian and the Merse; whilst in 1385, when the King of Scots was at Stirling, Edinburgh people referred to him as being "in the Highlands".' The Highlands, therefore, developed as a region of very scattered communities, independent-minded, lawless, with a separate language and culture and relatively ungovernable by a monarch based at Stirling, Fife or Edinburgh. A succession of rebellions inevitably took place. It was the mighty Somerled, lord of the Isles, who eventually drove the Norsemen out of the West Highlands. He became ruler of the west coast from Lewis to the Isle of Man and his power rivalled that of the monarch himself. A confrontation was inevitable, and in 1164, King Malcolm IV took the initiative and defeated Somerled's army at Renfrew, thus bringing Galloway under the Crown's control, but achieving no real authority over the Macdonald factions who followed their lord. The Norwegian fleet returned in 1263, but the Norsemen under Hakon IV were beaten back this time and for the last time by King Alexander III at the battle of Largs.

The kings of Scotland and the clans

The significant next stage in clan development took place in the fourteenth century, once Robert the Bruce had established himself as king of a united Scotland. Having eventually triumphed against the English with the support of many Highlanders, Bruce sought to implant firm government knowing that he still had enemies, and in feudal fashion he allocated land and power to those who had supported him. The influence of those who had sided with the English to oppose him, such as the house of Comyn, and the Macdougalls in the west, went into decline. However, the names of those who signed the Ragman Roll, giving forced homage to King Edward I of England as overlord in 1296, or the Declaration of Arbroath which petitioned the Pope to recognize an independent Scotland in 1320, clearly indicate the chiefly houses and names of Scotland that existed both before and after the war of independence.

Bruce, having united Scotland, was determined to keep it so, gifting responsibilities to those whom he believed would further his cause. Many of these, however, subsequently became strong and developed their own ideas – not exactly what Bruce had envisaged. His descendants, through his daughter Marjory's marriage to Walter, 6th High Steward of Scotland, in 1315, were to prove a turbulent, unsettled dynasty, reflecting the state of the land they ruled. Of the five Stewart kings who preceded Mary Queen of Scots, James I was murdered at Perth in 1473; James II was killed by a bursting cannon at the siege of Roxburgh in 1460; James III was killed at the battle of Sauchieburn in 1488; James IV was killed at the battle of Flodden in 1513; and James V died shortly after the rout of Solway Moss in 1542.

England never quite accepted that it did not have superiority over Scotland. The border, therefore, was a constant worry with raiding and reiving (ravaging, plundering) a way of life. Border families gained prominence as they were seen to be maintaining the safety of the realm. Families such as the house of Douglas, although constantly loyal, acquired lands and power to such an extent that they themselves were realized to be a threat to the ruling house of Stewart.

In the north, clan disputes and squabbles continued and it was these that led to Bruce's great-grandson, Alexander Stewart, the volatile brother of King Robert III, being appointed Lord High Justiciar of the North in 1372. Known as the Wolf of Badenoch, he was at that time married to the Countess of Buchan, heiress of one of the most ancient Celtic Mormaer titles, a marriage which brought him great influence, although he rapidly took steps to divorce her in favour of his mistress. From an impregnable island fortress on Lochindorb in Morayshire he imposed a ruthless grip of terror on those under his jurisdiction. Although he was officially removed from office, and was for a time excommunicated from the church by the Pope after he had burned Elgin Cathedral, he appears to have been remarkably successful in keeping the Highlands under control.

James IV made himself much beloved of his people by wandering among them in disguise to learn of their troubles. He crushed a rebellion in the Western Isles, and when he marched to battle against King Henry VIII of England in 1513, the best of the nation followed him to his death at Flodden. His granddaughter Mary spent six years of her tragic reign actually in Scotland, and by the time the crowns of England and Scotland became at last united in 1603 under her son, James VI and I, the Highland clans had already become very remote from government. When the court moved to London, this trend continued. It is interesting, however, to contemplate how the clans, as such, continued to be loyal to the person of the Ard Righ, the High King, although often indifferent to his government. It shows that the original clan concept remained consistent. When King Charles I was executed, it was to the Highlands that his son, later King Charles II, appealed for support. One of those who answered the call was James Graham, 1st Marquis of Montrose who, although at odds with the Sovereign's decrees concerning the Covenanters, remained loyal to the Sovereign's person. Montrose was a brilliant military strategist, understood the

THE ROYAL DYNASTIES OF SCOTLAND

From the merger of the Pictish and Celtic thrones

House of Alpin

843–60	Kenneth I MacAlpine
860–63	Donald I
863–77	Constantine
877–78	Aed
878–89	Eochaid
889–900	Donald II
900–42	Constantine II
942–50	Malcolm I
950–62	Indülf
962–67	Dubh
967–71	Colin or Cuilean
971–95	Kenneth II
995–97	Constantine III
997–1005	Kenneth III
1005–34	Malcolm II
1034–40	Duncan I
1040–57	MacBeth
1057–58	Lulach

House of Dunkeld

1058–93	Malcolm III Ceann Mor
1093–94	Donald Ban
1094	Duncan II
1094–97	Edmund
1097–1107	Edgar
1107–24	Alexander I

[The House of Dunkeld]

1124–53	David I
1153–65	Malcolm IV The Maiden
1165–1214	William, The Lion
1214–49	Alexander II
1249–86	Alexander III
1286–90	Margaret The Maid of Norway
1292–96	John Balliol

House of Bruce

1306–29	Robert I The Bruce
1329–71	David II

House of Stewart

1371–89	Robert II
1389–1406	Robert III
1406–37	James I
1437–60	James II
1460–88	James III
1488–1513	James IV
1513–42	James V

House of Stuart

1542–67	Mary Queen of Scots
1567–1625	James VI and James I of England
1625–49	Charles I
1649–60	The Commonwealth
1660–85	Charles II
1685–89	James II —— Jacobite Line
1689–1702	William and Mary
1702–14	Anne

House of Hanover

1714–27	George I
1727–60	George II
1760–1820	George III
1820–30	George IV
1830–37	William IV
1837–1901	Victoria

House of Saxe-Coburg-Gotha

1901–1910	Edward VII

House of Windsor

1910–36	George V
1936	Edward VIII
1936–52	George VI
1952–	Elizabeth I and II

LEFT *Mary, Queen of Scots*

BELOW *James VI and James I of England*

Highlanders' fighting abilities, and was certainly the first leader both to rally and employ them successfully. His failure ultimately came only through betrayal. But his achievements were indicative of what the Highland clans, properly mobilized, were capable of doing.

Hanoverians and Jacobites

There are periods in a country's history when remote events irrevocably determine the future. Such a time began for the Highlands of Scotland when a Protestant German prince was recruited to the British throne by a Whig Westminster government in 1714 in preference to a rightful Catholic claimant. In this they were acting in complete conformity with the Union Settlement of 1707 and, indeed, with the Act of the Scottish parliament of that same year ensuring a Protestant succession. First the son and then the grandson of the last of the Stuart monarchs, the deposed and exiled *de jure* King James VII and II, looked to Scotland for

ABOVE *Bonnie Prince Charlie, 'The Young Pretender'*

LEFT *James Francis Stuart, 'The Old Pretender'*

support. Thus the Jacobite cause was born. The claims of Prince James Francis, known as 'the Old Pretender', and Prince Charles Edward, 'the Young Pretender', the 'Kings across the Water', were justified, but not acceptable to the Church of England owing to their Catholic faith. In a Europe torn asunder by religious struggle, the Stuarts had found refuge at the court of Louis XIV of France for political rather than compassionate reasons. To begin with their cause had been championed by a France intent on overthrowing the Protestant William of Orange, married to James Francis' half-sister, Princess Mary, subsequently Queen Mary, and who had usurped the British throne. On the death of Queen Anne, the Catholic son of her half-brother was a more acceptable ally for France than a representative from the Protestant House of Hanover. All this had little to do with Scotland to begin with, but the idea of Jacobitism began to flourish, particularly with the unpopularity of the imported German king.

The first foray took place in 1715 when the Old Pretender landed at

Loch Sheil from Glenfinnan,
where Prince Charles Edward Stuart
rallied the Clans in 1745

Peterhead. The Stuarts' blue and gold standard was raised at Braemar by the Earl of Mar who had gathered an army of 5000 which speedily enlarged to 10,000 and consisted of Scottish nobles, chieftains and their kilted clansmen. Opposing them was the 2nd Duke of Argyll, chief of Clan Campbell and supporter of King George I.

Despite so much optimism at the start, the uprising was a disaster. The Jacobite forces, routed at Preston and Sheriffmuir, fled into the glens of the Highlands and disappeared. Six weeks after landing on Scottish soil, Prince James Francis fled from Montrose. The many impoverished refugees who followed him brought news of brutal reprisals inflicted on his supporters in the Highlands: 'Nothing but an entire desolation from Stirling to Inverness', wrote one Jacobite. Disconsolate in their failure, no longer welcome at Versailles, the Stuarts moved to Turin, Modena, and eventually to Rome.

Twenty-nine years later, a new Stuart Jacobite candidate stepped forward to claim his kingdom. Once more the timing seemed right; Hanoverian rule of Britain was widely held in contempt. Yet the second and final Jacobite rebellion was to take place with repercussions which would not only devastate the clan system, but irrevocably change every aspect of the Highland way of existence.

The 1745 uprising

Prince Charles Edward Stuart, aged twenty-five, arrived on the island of Eriskay in 1745. Having spent the night in a humble croft, he next day received Alexander Macdonald of Boisdale, who advised him to go home. 'I am home,' replied the Prince.

At Glenfinnan, at the head of Loch Sheil in Inverness-shire where the monument now stands, Charles Edward watched as the Duke of Atholl raised the Royal Standard and read out the Old Pretender's declaration in which Prince Charles Edward was appointed Regent of the Kingdom. On arrival, there had been only 150 Macdonalds to meet him. Two hours later, 700 Camerons led by Donald of Locheil appeared, then 300 more Macdonalds. In the weeks that followed support came from the Duke of Perth, Lord George Murray, Lord Ogilvy, Lord Strathallan, Lord Nairn, Macpherson of Cluny, Oliphant of Gask. Something of a dandy – although this does not imply that he was not an extremely tough young man, as he was to prove in the months to come – the young prince adopted a tartan suit trimmed in gold lace as a uniform. By the time he arrived in Edinburgh, he had captured the imagination of all who saw him. This colourful, handsome fair-haired prince with an army of kilted Highlanders determined to regain his father's rightful throne had instant appeal for those romantics who despised the fleshy, ageing King George II.

It is not relevant here to go into the details of the 1745 uprising, and suffice it to know that the course of events which culminated in Prince Charles Edward's defeat at Culloden Moor on 15 April 1746 had a great deal to do with the associations, developments and concepts attached to the clans and the wearing of tartan, and all that they symbolize for the Scot today scattered throughout the world.

Prince Charles Edward fled to Europe and died in obscurity in 1788, leaving an illegitimate daughter, the Duchess of Albany, and his Cardinal brother Henry as sole lawful heir to the Jacobite crown. As a prince of the Church of Rome, Henry died without lawful issue. At the time of his death his heir was the childless King of Sardinia, Charles Emmanuel IV, who was succeeded within a few months by his brother Victor Emmanuel I. They were great-grandsons of Victor Amadeus II, King of Sicily and Sardinia, who had married Anne Marie, daughter of Henrietta, Duchess of Orleans, younger sister of Charles II and James VII and II. The Cardinal King nominated Charles Emmanuel IV as his successor in his will of 1802.

Never again would a government in Britain tolerate an uprising of the clans in the north of Scotland. The power wielded by the chiefs was by now not only considered dangerous and anachronistic, it had to be smashed once and for always. The wearing of Highland dress, the tartan cloth which had become synonymous with rebellion, was outlawed.

Tartan at the crossroads

The Act of Proscription, 1746, followed a succession of complicated Acts designed to disarm the rebellious Highlanders. It stated:

From and after the first day of August, one thousand seven hundred and forty seven, no Man or Boy, within that part of Great Britain called Scotland, other than such as shall be employed as Officers and Soldiers in His Majesty's Forces, shall, on any pretence whatsoever wear or put on the Clothes commonly called Highland Clothes (that is to say) the Plaid, Philabeg, or little Kilt, Trowse, Shoulder Belts, or any part whatsoever of what peculiarly belongs to the Highland Garb; and that no Tartan, or party-coloured Plaid or Stuff shall be used for Great Coats, or for Upper Coats; and if any such Person shall presume after the first day of August, to wear or put on the aforesaid Garments, or any part of them, every such Person so offending, being convicted thereof by the Oath of One or more credible Witness or Witnesses before any Court of Justiciary or any one or more Justices of the Peace for the Shire or Stewartry, or Judge Ordinary of the Place where such Offence shall be committed, shall suffer imprisonment, without Bail, during the space of Six Months, and no longer; and that being convicted for a second Offence before a Court of Justiciary, or at the Circuits, shall be liable to be transported to any of His Majesty's Plantations beyond the Seas, there to remain for the space of Seven Years.

This was pretty tough treatment for wearing patterned cloth which had been worn by simple Highland folk for centuries. The purpose of the various Acts then was clear; they sought to destroy the unity of the Highland clanspeople and to bring them in line with the people of the Lowlands. Although the benign Lord President Forbes, who did more than any other to persuade the Hanoverian government towards more humane behaviour after Culloden, described the Bill for altering Highland dress as 'no more than a chip in porridge', there were those who saw it as fundamental to stamping out the 'military' uniform of a minority rebellion and maintaining law and order.

In his *History of Highland Dress*, 1962, John Telfer Dunbar quotes Lord President Forbes' plea to the Lord Lyon in July 1746:

The Garb is certainly very loose and fits men inured to it, to go through Great Fatigues, to make very quick Marches, to bear out against the Inclemency of the Weather, to wade through Rivers and shelter in Huts, Woods and Rocks upon occasion: which Men dress'd in the Low Country Garb could not possibly endure. But then it is to be considered, that as the Highlands are circumstanced at present, it is, at least it seems to me to be, an Utter impossibility, without the advantage of this Dress, for the Inhabitants to tend their Cattle, and to go through the other parts of their Business, without which they could not subsist; not to speak of paying Rents to their Landlords.

*Cardinal York,
after P. Batoni
(detail)*

Forbes was deliberately being dramatic, but he obviously was concerned about the situation. The problem could possibly be compared with that of the British Raj insisting that Indians or Malays working in the fields should wear trousers and shoes instead of their practical native dress. However, the form and make-up of attire was not what occasioned the real problem. It was a belief that the varied patterns of tartan available at this time represented clan allegiances, and it was the continuance and exploitation of this belief in the following centuries that has led to an amazing amount of misrepresentation, not to say indulgent idiocy, being expended on the subject. In all the available antiquarian documentation concerning Highland dress before 1745, there is little clear indication that specific patterns used in the manufacture of plaid were exclusive to specific families. After the rebellions, the attire itself was associated with *all* the rebellious clans and deemed offensive. The patterns of material involved in that attire were not singled out individually, but as a whole. And it is almost certainly true to say that the ordinary Highlander would have worn a suitable and available 'district' cloth for his everyday clothes, whereas the more fashion-conscious and sophisticated might have selected a tartan design and colours in much the same way as another would select a tweed.

There is, however, evidence that 'district' tartan did become associated as 'clan' tartan, since those of a particular area where a particular design of cloth was manufactured were most likely to be of the same kin. Martin Martin, MacLeod of MacLeod's factor, who published his *Description of the Western Islands of Scotland* in 1703, had observed: 'Every isle differs from each other in their fancy of making plads, as to the stripes and Breadth and Colours. This Humour is as different thro the main land of the Highlands in-so-far that they who have seen those places, are able, at the first view of a man's plad, to guess the place of his residence . . .'

The origins of tartan

Telfer Dunbar makes the observation: 'In attempting to give the Highland dress in general – and tartan in particular – an antiquity which it cannot claim, some writers will even draw out attention to references a thousand years old. In fact, the early Christian costume of a loose shirt-like garment with an outer covering was universal and by no means restricted to the Gael.'

In the Magnus Barefoot Saga of 1093 there is reference to 'short kyrtles and upper garments' and through all the writings thereafter we can learn something of the mode of dress, but nothing specific about tartan cloth. Highlanders were described as 'savages' by many commenting on the bareness of their legs and general nakedness. As Lord President Forbes rightly implied, Highland attire was for practical everyday usage, not for any decorative or symbolic purpose.

Yet we do know that striped cloth of a sort was worn at a very early stage. The first credible reference, however, appears in the Lord High Treasurer's Accounts of 1538 where reference is made to an outfit of 'Heland tartane' for King James V. Further evidence comes from the French historian Beaugue, who refers to 'light covering of wool of many colours' at the siege of Haddington in 1548. The cloth, it appears, was manufactured from the wool of the now extinct Highland sheep, a long and fine-fleeced creature, whose coat was ideal for spinning into a fine hard thread. Supposedly it was spun using a spindle by the women of the glen. Colours came from the various plants in the vicinity. Martin Martin commented: 'The Women are at great pains, first to give an exact Pattern of the Plad upon a piece of wood having the number of every Thred of the Stripe upon it.' In 1587, a Charter granted Hector MacLean, Heir of Duart, lands in Islay, the feu duty to be payable in the form of 60 ells cloth of white, black and green colours which correspond with the hunting tartan of the house of Duart. It can therefore be assumed that the pattern became associated with the clan since it was manufactured in their territory. On another count, however, we have the ten Grant portraits at Cullen House painted by Richard Waite in the early eighteenth century where each brother is wearing a different tartan, and, where a coat and a plaid are worn, these also differ.

Sir Thomas Innes, when commenting on the tribal significance of tartan, refers to a letter from Sir Robert Gordon of Gordonstoun, then Tutor of Sutherland, to Murray of Pulrossie in 1618, 'requesting him to furl his pennon [standard or flag] when the Earl of Sutherland's banner was displayed and to remove the red and white lines from the plaids of his men so as to bring their dress into harmony with that of the other septs.'

This, states Sir Thomas, not only illustrates the close relation of heraldry to clanship, but that the tartan had by then a clan significance. It would seem that the Gordon Earls of Sutherland had already adopted the modern 'dark' tartan, designed to obliterate the bright stripes of the

older tartans; and also, no doubt, to eliminate so far as possible traces of the older tribal divisions, and to bring all their followers under the immediate sway of the Earls.

The matter, he continues, has an even greater significance, for the Murrays and Sutherlands were of similar origin, and if they were (as it appears) both wearing a dark-based tartan with red and white over-check – and Pulrossie's tartan was evidently very like what is known as 'Sutherland ancient' – then the parent check could date back to the twelfth or thirteenth century. This indeed may seem indicated from the sett termed 'Murray of Atholl', which has a similar background hue with a red overstripe, while the northern Murrays evidently had red and white. It looks as if Murray, Murray of Atholl and Sutherland ancient had a common origin in a sett basically used in the de Moravia tribe from the twelfth century. It was no doubt 'the Murrays' tartan' without being consciously '*the* Murray tartan'.

During the thirty-six years when the wearing of tartan was illegal, there were numerous minor incidents when offenders were taken into custody. Indeed, there was the strange case of the black servant of Stewart of Appin imprisoned for wearing tartan livery. Nevertheless, it was a period when the weaving and distribution of tartan cloth inevitably dropped away. Such significance as certain designs might have had for certain people in specific areas became vague; and records were not kept, for this was very much a simple craft industry.

ABOVE *Edinburgh Castle*

LEFT *Holyrood Palace, Edinburgh*

The tartan revival

By 1782, the Act was seen for what it was – absurd and ineffective; although it could be said that it had achieved its purpose and obscured the potential role of Highland dress as a clan uniform. Fashion had taken over and the nondescript, uniform grey clothing of the south had been imposed.

Through the efforts of the Duke of Montrose, the Act of Proscription was repealed. There then began a curious period when the costume, once reviled as the symbol of rebellion, became regarded as high fashion in both Scotland *and* England.

Since the early seventeenth century Highland Independent Companies had carried out military control duties and, in 1739, the Highland Regiment, later the Black Watch, was founded. During the Forty-five it fought for the Government, and because of this, during

31

proscription, their uniform was the only Highland costume that could legally be worn.

Thus it was that this regimental dress became the main link back with that of the past. The performance of the Black Watch at Waterloo against Napoleon heightened the reputation of the Scottish fighting man, so that his uniform became the subject of great interest both at home and in Continental Europe. Sir Walter Scott, whose novels conjured up the very romantic images which the Hanoverians of the Forty-five had sought to destroy, took an active part in organizing a levee for His Majesty King George IV when he visited Edinburgh in 1822. There is no doubt that this great occasion – the first visit by a Hanoverian reigning monarch to Scotland – was the biggest factor in the upsurge of interest in tartan. In collaboration with Stewart of Garth, Scott stage-managed the affair so adroitly that it was described by John Lockhart as Celtic 'hallucination'. Sir Thomas Innes quotes Sir Walter in his welcome to King George IV:

He is our kinsman. It is not too much to say that there is scarcely a gentleman of any kind of the old Scottish families who cannot 'count kin' with the Royal House from which our Sovereign is descended. In this small country blood has so intermingled that far the greatest part of our burgesses and yeomen are entitled to entertain similar pretensions. In short, we are *the clan* and our King is *the chief*. Let us remember that it is so; and not only look towards him as a father but to each other as if we were, in the words of the old song, 'Ae man's bairns'.

Sir Thomas refers to Erasmus' observation of the Scots that, 'Their habit is to make great boast of their birth, and to claim kindred with the Royal Family.' This Sir Thomas justifies:

Hardly is there a Scot today who cannot in some line of ancestry connect himself with the Royal line of Fergus Mor McEarc, and claim as a kinsman our Sovereign. This sense of kinship, the bond between the Ard Righ Albann and the great Peers and Chiefs, between these and the duine-uasail, and between the latter and the clan, has had a most far-reaching effect upon our Scottish civilization; for between the Peerage, the Houses of Chiefs and Chieftains, the Baronage, the Gudemen or Lesser Lairds and Tacksmen, it has been calculated that at the time of the Union there were (in a population of about a million) over ten thousand titled houses, each as proud and as nobly descended as any of the great Continental noblesses. Allowing for the expansion of even the near circle of these houses and lines of chieftains, it follows that about 1 in each 45 people were actually members of a titled or chiefly house, and that about one half of the Scottish nation consciously regarded themselves as members of the aristocracy. Such a proportion is unknown in any other nation, and the moral and social effect upon the Scottish nation has been incalculable. Under the clan system, the lines of chiefs and chieftains were regarded as pegs upon which hung the glory of the whole race or sept, and their pedigree, preserved by the clan bards and historians, was treasured as the common pride of all the descendants of their line. But in this system no attempt was made to found a noble caste, public-school caste, or snobbery of that description, and the younger members were expected by degrees to subside in an ever-

OPPOSITE *George* IV
by David Wilkie

extending pyramid into the duine-uasail and body of the clan, carrying with them through all ranks of the nation the pride and glory of lineage and achievement, and the sense of acknowledged blood-brotherhood upon either side, stretching throughout the whole gamut of the Caledonian social system.

There are attributes which can only be perfected when inheritance is coupled with a favourable environment, and these highest social assets are not perfectly preserved beyond three or four generations, when separated from the conditions in which they flourish: hence the national importance of a steadily continuing but non-caste aristocracy which sets the style and character of a nation. Through the Celtic system, in whose lines of chiefs, chieftains and peers these attributes were developed, these benefits were, as by a refreshing stream, spread through the ranks of each clan and house. Thus it is that in Scotland no servile yokels of the rural English or Continental type are found in the Highland glens; and the clansmen reared in the crofts and cottages bore, and in most parts still carry with them, the old pride of race and of a glorious past. So it is that the clansman has so often risen, when chance or circumstances favoured, from herding the kine in some peaceful Highland glen to take his place as an equal, and not as a parvenu, amongst the princes and statesmen of the Continent, or has with calm and graceful confidence assumed the direction of vast enterprise throughout the Empire.

Clanship and the Scots' instinct of belonging to a tribal grouping, the maintenance of subinfeudation, which the Plantagenets abolished in England, and the incorporation of many older Celtic customary provisions, made Scottish feudalism the means of perpetuating the hundreds of tiny Celtic provincial states or clan territories which together form the Realm of Scotland. These 'little countries', each of which originally formed an alloidial or *duthus* unit, held free of rent or service, were gradually resigned to the Ard Righ Albann (the High King of Scotland who thus became a feudal overlord) to be held on tenure which it was fondly believed would give a greater security to those who had, in the words of one of the old clan historians, 'first raised fire or boiled water upon these lands'; a tenure which would, in the language of a celebrated charter granted by Macdonald to one of his vassals of the Isles, endure 'so long as the waves should beat upon the rock'.

The great deception

In the wake of the enthusiasm inspired by Sir Walter Scott and his followers at the beginning of the nineteenth century came certain influences that were to muddle and manipulate the wearing of Highland dress up until recent times when historians with no commercial, political or poetical axes to grind have sought to put the records straight.

The most notable exploiters were two brothers, John Sobieski Stolberg Stuart Hay and his younger brother Charles Edward. It is understood that they were the sons of one Thomas Allen, himself the son of Admiral John Carter Allen. The Stuart Hay brothers' claim was that their father, born in Italy, was the legitimate son of Prince Charles Edward Stuart by his wife Princess Louisa of Stolberg Gedern. The name of Sobieski comes from Prince Charles Edward's mother who belonged to the Sobieska Royal House of Poland. The brothers claimed that their father had been adopted by Admiral Allen in order to protect him and that his birth had been kept a secret.

There are variations on this story, but what seems quite indicative of the romantic sentimentality of the time is that most of those to whom this fable was revealed were quite prepared to believe it. It seems the brothers were readily welcomed into social circles in both London and Edinburgh. In 1829, seven years after King George IV had visited Edinburgh and Scotland had rediscovered a past filled with noble, tartan-clad fantasy, the Sobieski brothers dropped a tartan bombshell. They publicly revealed that they had in their possession the so-called Cromarty Manuscript, a book that consisted of twenty-eight pages devoted to the subject of tartan and bearing the date 1721. They insisted that it was based on a sixteenth-century publication held by their father and acquired from the Scots College of Douai in France. The Cromarty Manuscript was said to have been written by one Sir Richard Urquhart, an elusive, if not fictitious character.

Sir Thomas Dick Lauder, a Morayshire landowner, was a friend of the Stuart Hay brothers and Sir Walter Scott. In his *History of Highland Dress*, John Telfer Dunbar quotes from letters he had acquired in which Sir Thomas first raises the subject with Sir Walter:

I hear that tartans were some centuries ago in use universally over Scotland, and accordingly the author of the Manuscript after giving us first descriptions of thirty-eight different Tartans belonging to the principal Highland families and of 'The tartinies of lesser famylies or houses the quhilk be command from the cheff gouses and original clannes' goes on with 'Here begynne the off the Laich Cuntrie Pairtes and Border Clannes' of which families he gives us the descriptions of twenty-eight tartans, among these last you may believe the Tartan of the illustrious family of Scott is not forgotten. The descriptions are all so very particular that it is quite impossible to mistake them, and as I wished to possess myself of a copy of the Manuscript (which I wrote out myself) Mr Charles Stuart Hay with very great politeness agreed to illuminate it for me with drawings of all the Tartans, a work which occupied him unceasingly for above three weeks by which labour he has made me a most beautiful book. There is no printed copy of the manuscript. But the Messrs Hay Junior are in possession of a manuscript copy which is very old.

Sir Walter wrote back firmly insisting that the original manuscript be sent to Register House so that authenticity could be proved. He was obviously sceptical, observing:

The general proposition that the Lowlanders ever wore plaids is difficult to swallow. They were of twenty different races, and almost all distinctly different from the Scots Irish, who are the proper Scots, from which the Royal Family are descended. For instance, there is scarce a great family in the Lowlands of Scotland that is not to be traced to the Normans, the proudest as well as the most civilized race in the eleventh and twelfth centuries. Is it natural to think that holding the Scots in the contempt in which they did, they would have adopted their dress? If you will look at Bruce's speech to David II, as the historian Aelred tells the story, you will see he talks of the Scots as a British officer would do of the Cherokees. Or take our country, the central and western part of the Border; it was British, Welsh if you please, with the language and manners of that people who certainly wore no tartan. It is needless to prosecute this, though I could show, I think, that there is no period in Scottish history when manners, language or dress of the Highlanders were adopted in the Low Country.

Sir Walter was not entirely dismissive. He must have been aware that tartan of a sort, variations on the kilt and even the traditional bagpipes had been reported observed in other corners of the Celtic, or allegedly Celtic, world – in the Basque areas of Spain; in Ireland, naturally, and indeed in Albania.

All the evidence, however, points to the Stuart Hay brothers' revelations as being a total fabrication and it may be wondered if they fully appreciated what they were starting. The original Cromarty Manuscript was in the possession of Thomas Allen, who apparently refused to part with it, so it never was sent to Register House to be authenticated. In the meantime, Sir Thomas and Sir Walter continued to correspond on the subject, and Sir Walter makes one particularly interesting observation: 'The idea of distinguishing the clans by their tartans is but a fashion of modern date in the Highlands themselves; much less could it be supposed to be carried to such an extent in the Lowlands as the manuscript pretends. Tartan itself is unquestionably a Lowland word, and the stuff "tiertain" fetched from Flanders, and I suspect the Highlanders wore a frieze mantle like the Irish chief, without what we call the bracken.'

In 1845, the Stuart Hay brothers published *Vestiarium Scoticum*: from the manuscript formerly in the library of the Scots College at Douai; with an introduction and notes. This extraordinary book was very large and weighed over twenty pounds. It illustrated seventy-five tartans in full colour, nearly all of which were unknown to manufacturers of the time, but soon became popular to the extent that they are widely known and recognized today as 'official' clan and family tartans.

The authors were widely criticized at the time and thereafter, but the fact remains that they had brilliantly exploited a situation where there was an almost irrational social demand by families wanting to claim their own exclusive tartans based on the national dress of Scotland. No trace of the Douai manuscript exists today. Towards the end of the nineteenth century, the Cromarty Manuscript was submitted by its owner for chemical analysis. The opinion given was that there was evidence of chemical treatment designed to age the paper. Conveniently for some, the manuscript then disappeared, giving credence to the supposition that it was most certainly a fake. Be that as it may, throughout Queen Victoria's reign and up until the present day, tartan developed into big business. Clan and family tartans became an integral part of the whole concept of being Scottish.

The wearing and usage of tartan

Sir Iain Moncreiffe, as great an expert as there is ever likely to be on the subject, put it as follows:

Apparently there were and are no rules about which tartan to wear and who should wear it, except those which have arisen through courteous convention, and those governing its use as uniform. By the time of the Union in 1707, tartan was worn all over Scotland, but the standard setts of today's tartans were not, as such, in general use in the highlands much before family tartans were adopted to distinguish the great lowland names. So people should not bother over much whether their tartan is Highland or Lowland, 20th or 19th or even only just 18th century. The whole certain period of nearly all the meaningful tartans now in existence is comparatively short.

Nowadays, however, tartans are recorded in the Court of the Lord Lyon in Edinburgh. Here records are kept to protect the thread count of individual patterns. However, this is not in order to ensure that the manufacture is exclusive and thereby controlled for some élitist purpose, but to preserve the individuality of each clan or family pattern. And aside from this, there are no specific laws governing the wearing or usage of tartan other than those of courtesy and respect for a national institution. Purists will argue angrily on topics such as kilt lengths and quote a number of rather extraordinary theories derived from patently eccentric Victorian sources. Be that as it may, the fact remains that tartan is one of the most brilliant decorative concepts and the author of this book entirely endorses its use in all kinds of situations. There is no

Queen Victoria and family exploring the Highlands on Shetland ponies

reason why Queen Victoria's example should not be followed and tartan designs used for carpets, wallcoverings and furnishing fabrics: such usage does not belittle tartan and need not be considered as kitsch – it is all a question of taste.

There would also appear to be no reason why tartans should not be mixed, providing that the colours do not clash and that the wearer has some legitimate claim to them. There are examples of such mixing of tartans illustrated in family portraits executed before the Forty-five, although it is not suggested that wearers go to the extremes illustrated by R. R. McIan in his fanciful commissions for the Highland Society in 1845. But the advent of tartan trousers as part of the Punk Rock cult of the late 1970s represented an interesting concept. Highland costume can be both innovative and flamboyant, and its materials can be adapted to popular modern fashions.

Clans in the twentieth century

The traditional myths about the Clans of the Highlands of Scotland can easily be challenged by the truth concerning the Highland Clearances which took place steadily throughout the second half of the eighteenth century and well into the nineteenth century. Families starved, evicted, dispossessed and deported make a nonsense of the noble, paternalistic sentiment associated with the clan system. It must therefore be conceded that the Rebellion of 1745 was the final watershed for the clans as such, for when the Highlanders departed from the glens and mountains of the north of Scotland and were forced to seek such fortune as could be found in Glasgow, the United States, Canada, Australia and New Zealand, they left behind them vast acres of uninhabited land that to this day has not recovered any realistic economic viability. However, with the native tenacity of their race, the Scots in the New World succeeded in creating a future not so much for the old-style clan, but for a remarkable international bond of kinship which has found a powerful following in the twentieth century. Throughout the world Scottish descent is claimed by millions with a pride not at all dissimilar to the spirit which resulted in Robert the Bruce's tumultuous victory over the English at Bannockburn in 1314.

In the United States, for example, there are over seventy-two Scottish celebrations which take place in the course of each year. The most impressive of these are the games held at Grandfather Mountain in North Carolina in July, and at Stone Mountain in Atlanta, Georgia, in October. At the University of Old Dominion, Virginia, there is an annual Festival of Scottish Culture; in Texas there are international gatherings. There are organizations such as the Association of Scottish Clans of America, Inc., founded by Doctor Herbert P. McNeal; Scottish Heritage in New York; and, in Canada, CASSOC (Clans and Scottish Societies of Canada) and the Sons of Scotia. Traditional Scottish sports – tossing the caber, throwing the hammer, Scottish wrestling – are popular. Pipe bands are legion; Scottish fiddle music and the clarsach attract many enthusiasts; and Scottish Country Dancing has survived in a far more serious and respected form than it is often practised in the homeland.

A classic example of how the Scots have effortlessly integrated with their adopted countries is found in the American South where, some generations ago, one William McIntosh married the Princess of the Creek Nation. His descendants, as hereditary chiefs of the Creek Nation, not only maintain the tradition of wearing the full eagle feather headdress on ceremonial occasions, but often wear the Mackintosh kilt as well.

In 1977, the International Gathering Trust was created in Edinburgh to promote Scottish Gatherings not only in Scotland, but across the world. In the following year, Queen Elizabeth the Queen Mother attended a gathering in Nova Scotia, and Australia, California and Chicago have made plans for similar projects. One feature of such events in the various countries is that you find people of the same name and origins from completely different parts of the world rediscovering their family links. In Novia Scotia, Mackenzies from Canada, America, Scotland, Hawaii and Germany came together for the first time and were astonished at the facial similarities. As the network grows around the world, its influence increases. The Scots never were a people who co-existed comfortably in the limiting yet competitive confines of Scotland itself. But scattered around the world and representing forceful and successful ethnic communities within their chosen countries, they must surely be counted a force to be reckoned with.

SCOTLAND OF OLD

compiled by the late Sir Iain Moncreiffe of that Ilk

The lands shown for each name indicate general spheres of influence, usually about the time of King James VI of Scotland but taking the history of each district or family as a whole.

The numbers on the map relate to the accompanying list and are of smaller areas or former seats held by that family.

6 Baillie of Lamington
8 Balfour of Balfour
9 Barclay of Towie
10 Beaton of Balfour
13 Boyd, Earl of Kilmarnock
17 Bruce, Earl of Elgin
19 Buchanan of that Ilk

26 Cathcart, Earl of Cathcart
27 Charteris of Amisfield
28 The Captain of Clan Chattan
29 Cheyne of Esslemont
32 Cockburn of Langton

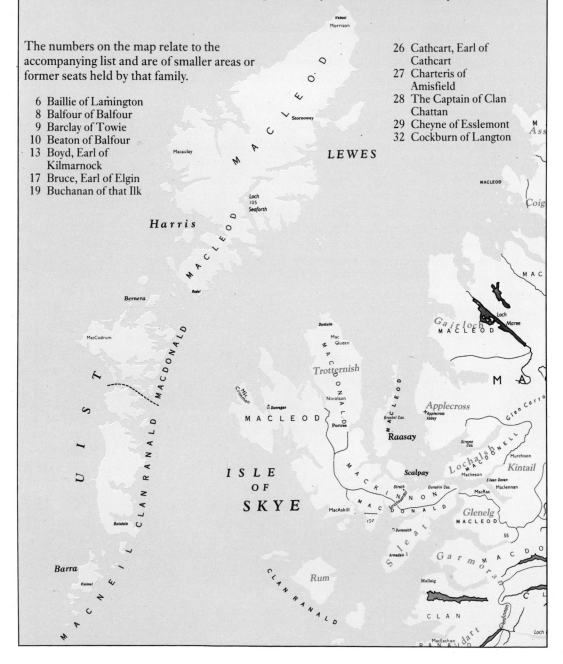

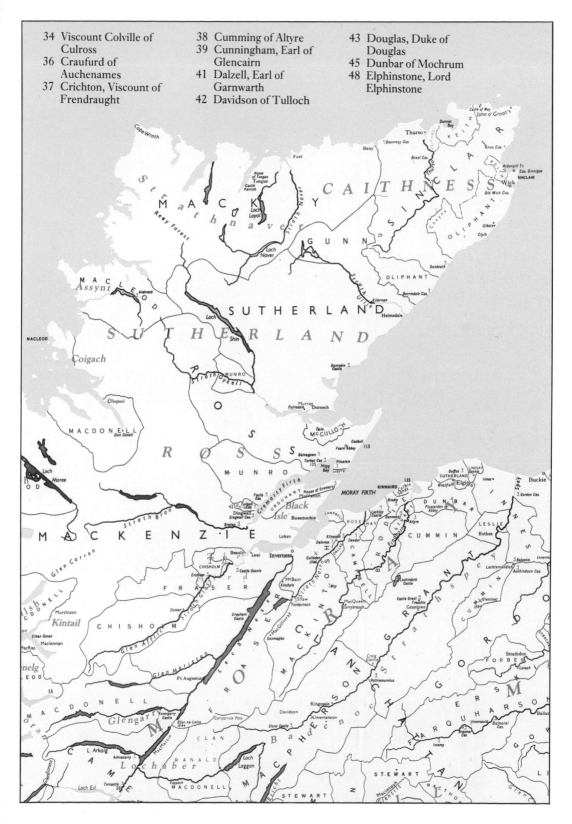

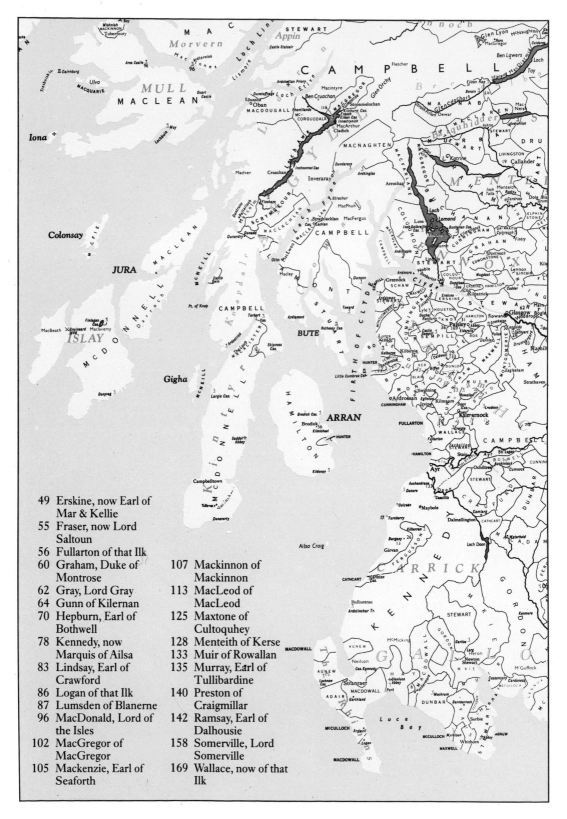

49 Erskine, now Earl of Mar & Kellie
55 Fraser, now Lord Saltoun
56 Fullarton of that Ilk
60 Graham, Duke of Montrose
62 Gray, Lord Gray
64 Gunn of Kilernan
70 Hepburn, Earl of Bothwell
78 Kennedy, now Marquis of Ailsa
83 Lindsay, Earl of Crawford
86 Logan of that Ilk
87 Lumsden of Blanerne
96 MacDonald, Lord of the Isles
102 MacGregor of MacGregor
105 Mackenzie, Earl of Seaforth

107 Mackinnon of Mackinnon
113 MacLeod of MacLeod
125 Maxtone of Cultoquhey
128 Menteith of Kerse
133 Muir of Rowallan
135 Murray, Earl of Tullibardine
140 Preston of Craigmillar
142 Ramsay, Earl of Dalhousie
158 Somerville, Lord Somerville
169 Wallace, now of that Ilk

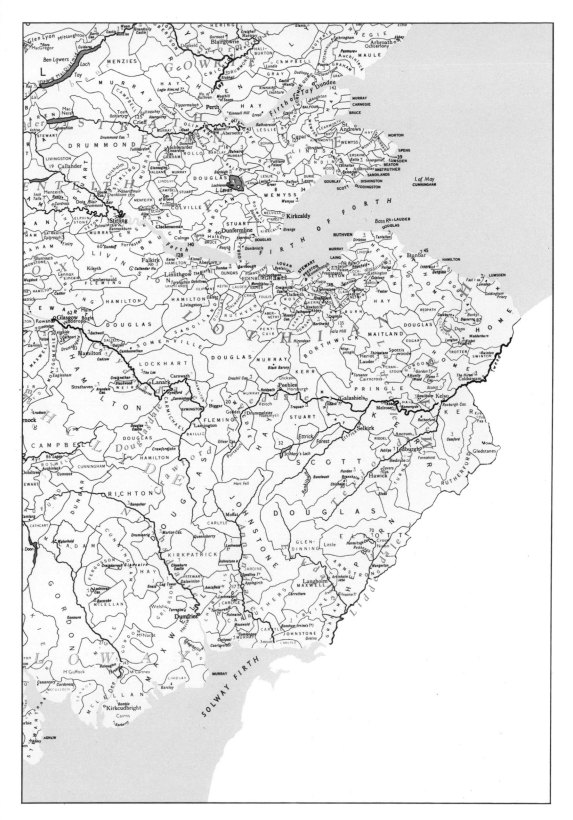

43

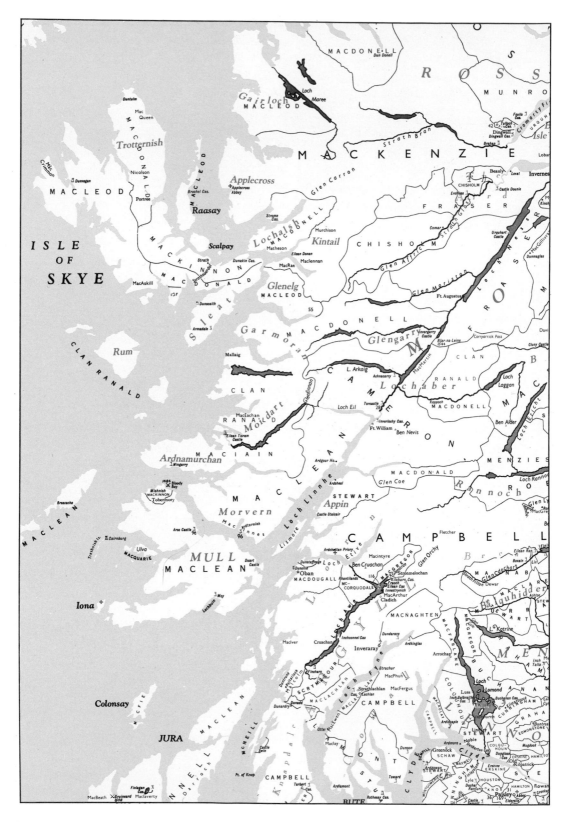

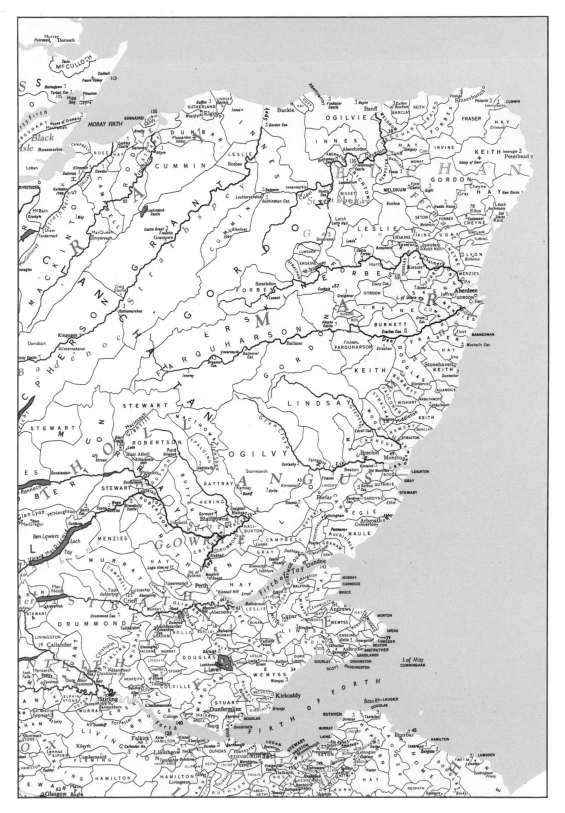

SCOTTISH CLAN AND
FAMILY NAMES
AND THEIR SEPTS

*The Royal Arms as on Her Majesty's
Great Seal for Scotland*

SCOTTISH
FAMILY NAMES

Abercrombie

THE NAME comes from the barony of Aber-cromby in Fife, and its first recorded bearer is William de Abercromby in 1296. The Abercrombies of that Ilk, the premier family of that name, became extinct in the middle of the seventeenth century, and the Abercrombies of Birkenbog took over as representatives of the name. Members of the family served in the Garde Ecossaise in France.

Sir, Alexander, 1st Baron of Birkenbog (1636) was a Commissioner for Banffshire. His son sat as MP for Banff in the Scottish Parliament of 1694.

Abernethy

REPRESENTATIVES of this name were lay abbots of the Culdee monastery of Abernethy in Strathearn. The very first recorded Abernethy is Hugh, who lived in the twelfth century. His son was Orm de Abernethy and there is evidence to suggest that he received lands at Ormiston, East Lothian.

Abernthys appear in Upper Lauderdale in the thirteenth century, probably as vassals of the de Morevilles.

The family of Abernethy enjoyed the 'privilege of sanctuary'. In pre-Reformation Scotland certain churches were recognized as asylums for fugitives from justice. Such persons could take refuge in a sanctuary and be safe from punishment unless their crime was sacrilege or treason, but they would have to repent and accept punishment of sorts. All religious sanctuaries were abolished in Scotland at the Reformation in 1560. The Abernethys, therefore, until the mid-sixteenth century, could claim impunity in this way.

Lord Abernethy is a title held by the Duke of Hamilton and Brandon.

Agnew

THE FIRST RECORD of the name in Scotland appears in Liddesdale around 1190, when William des Aigneu witnessed a charter between Ranulf de Soulis and Jedburgh Abbey. The family are of Norman origin taking the name from the Barony d'Agneaux.

In 1363 the Lochnaw family of the name were appointed hereditary sheriffs of Galloway by David II. In 1426, Andrew Agnew was appointed Constable of Lochnaw Castle. Sir Patrick, 8th Sheriff, was created a Baronet of Nova Scotia.

A branch of the family went to Ulster and obtained grants of lands near Larne from James VI. Their castle of Kilwaughter is now a ruin, but many families in the United States and Australia descend from this line.

Sir Crispin Agnew of Lochnaw, Baronet, is Unicorn Pursuivant at the Court of the Lord Lyon.

Agnew

49

The ancient stronghold of Lochnaw Castle, Dumfries and Galloway, dates from the thirteenth century, but is now a ruin. There is a fifteenth-century castle on the shores of the loch and an Agnew Mausoleum in old Leswalt kirkyard.

Anderson or MacAndrew

THIS SURNAME is connected with St Andrew, the patron saint of Scotland. The name means 'Son of Andrew' and the cross of St Andrew is shown on the shields carried by the Andersons. The name is common in Aberdeenshire, where Andersons or MacAndrews are generally thought to be connected with the Clan Anrias, a sept of Clan Ross. Clan Anrias settled in Connage of Petty on the Moray Firth and became associated with the Clan Chattan federation, particularly with the Mackintoshes.

Prominent branches of Clan Anderson are the Andersons of Dowhill, of Wester Ardbreck in Banffshire, and of Candacraig in Strathdon. Arms were awarded in the sixteenth century to Anderson of that Ilk, but his family has not yet been identified and, as a result, the chiefship has been dormant.

Anderson

In 1748, the mentally unstable widow of a soldier returned to her home town of Elgin and gave birth to a son in the lavatory of the cathedral. This child grew up to become Lieutenant-General Anderson and when he died bequeathed part of his considerable fortune to the town. One of Scotland's most distinguished architects was Row and Anderson, and the singer Moira Anderson is famous the world over for her interpretation of Scottish songs.

Angus

THE NAME means 'Unique Choice' and an Angus was King of Dalriada in western Scotland in the ninth century. The name is associated with Clan MacInnes, who are believed to have evolved from the Dalriada Scots.

Moira Anderson, the Scottish soprano who is known the world over for her songs of Scotland

At Athelstaneford, north-east of Haddington in East Lothian, Angus (d. 761), son of Fergus, King of the Picts, engaged in battles against the Scots, Britons and Angles. Legend has it that he won a great victory through the intervention of St Andrew when a white cross formation of clouds was seen in the sky.

The Earldom of Angus was held by the Stewarts and Douglases and is now vested in the Dukedom of Hamilton. Lands of Abernethy were owned by Earls of Angus of various families.

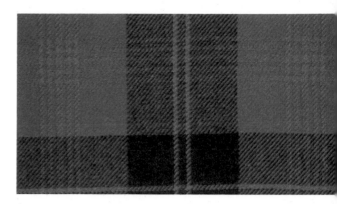

Angus

Anstruther

FROM THE LANDS of Anstruther in Fife which incorporate the famous fishing village of that name. The barony was held by the de Candelas, a Norman family who had lands in Dorset in the twelfth century, and William de Candela assumed the territorial designation of Anstruther. A David Anstruther served with the Garde Ecossaise of France and his descendants are the barons of Anstrude of the seigniory of Barry.

Sir Robert Anstruther, 1st Baronet, purchased Balcaskie in Fife in 1698. The 5th and 6th Baronets were Lord-Lieutenants of Fife. Sir James Anstruther was appointed Hereditary Carver by James VI and I. The present Chief, Sir Ralph Anstruther of Anstruther and Balcaskie, Bt, CVO, MC, became Treasurer and Equerry to Queen Elizabeth the Queen Mother.

Arbuthnott

THE SURNAME originates from Berwickshire where it was adopted by Duncan, son and heir of Hugh of Swinton, who had received the lands of Arbuthnott in Kincardineshire from Walter Olifard at the end of the twelfth century. The family still hold these lands which were granted to Olifard by William the Lion around 1175, almost certainly as a knight's fee.

Arbuthnott House is situated 8 miles south-west of Stonehaven and before the sixteenth cen-

Arbuthnott

tury consisted of a thirteenth-century tower. The name is found in quantity around Peterhead, Grampian, and Adam Arbuthnot, a merchant in that town, bequeathed the local museum.

Armstrong

THERE IS a traditional story that the progenitor of the Armstrongs was the armour bearer to a king of Scots and rescued his monarch in the midst of battle when his horse was killed under him. From this deed, the family came to be known as 'Armstrong' and received a gift of lands in Liddesdale. The first chief of the name is Alexander, who held the seat of Mangerton in the late thirteenth century. In 1363 Gilbert Armstrong, Steward of the Household to

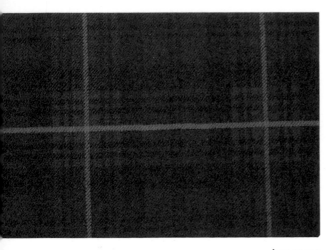

Armstrong

Baillie of Polkemmet

King David II, was Scotland's ambassador to England, and the family grew to become not only very powerful in the Borders of Scotland, but extremely turbulent, renowned as 'reivers' who made constant forays into England to raid and plunder.

In 1530 Johnnie Armstrong of Gilnockie who lived at Holehouse, otherwise known as Hollows Tower or Gilnockie Tower, 12 miles from Newcastleton, was invited to meet the young King James V, who seized him and his followers and hanged them. The family never recovered and with the death of the 10th Chief in 1610, the clan generally scattered.

On 21 July 1969, Neil Armstrong, an American descendant, became the first man to walk on the Moon; and he carried with him a fragment of Armstrong tartan. The first gathering of Armstrongs for nearly 400 years was held at the Tourneyholm in Liddesdale in 1979.

Baillie

DERIVED FROM the bailie or bailiff and not, as is believed by some, from Baliol. There are a number of prominent families of the name, notably those of Lamington, Polkemmet, Jerviswood and Dochfour. The Baillies of Dunain are believed to have been founded by a younger son of the house of Lamington.

Through the marriage of Colonel James Baillie,

Member of Parliament for Inverness, and Nellie Lisa Bass in 1894, the title of Baron Burton came into the Dochfour family.

Bain

THE DE BAYNS were found in England in the thirteenth century, but this is a well-distributed Scottish name. In the sixteenth century there were several to be found in St Andrews. The name is also found in Edinburgh, Dysart and Aberdeen in the seventeenth century. It occurs as a sept name of Clan

Mackay and, obviously, of Clan MacBain who settled in eastern Inverness-shire.

Baird

THE NAME originates from 'bard' meaning 'poet'. It was a Baird who rescued the Scottish King William the Lion from being savaged by a wild boar, and he was rewarded with grants of land. Robert, son of Waldave de Biggar, granted a Charter to Richard Baird of Meikle and Little Kyp in Lanarkshire in the thirteenth century, and Robert Bruce granted the barony of Cambuskenneth to one Robert Baird.

The surname appears in the Lothians and in Aberdeenshire in the fourteenth century and the family acquired Auchmeddan, 3 miles north of New Aberdour. There is a curious prophecy from Thomas the Rhymer that when the eagles that

John Logie Baird, the television pioneer who was born in Helensburgh in 1888

Arthur James Balfour, British Prime Minister from 1902 to 1905

nested in the crags there disappeared, the estate would pass from the Baird family. This came true when the estate was bought by the Earl of Aberdeen. The eagles returned when the Earl's heir married General Baird's sister, but disappeared again when the estate passed to the Gordons. General Sir David Baird was noted for his exploits in India, and in the expedition to recapture the Cape of Good Hope. He lost an arm at the battle of Corunna in 1809.

James Baird of Byth was created Baron Deveron by Charles I, but he died before the patent passed the Great Seal. His second son was created Sir Robert Baird of Saughton Hall and his eldest son, Lord Newbyth, was a Lord of Justiciary. John Logie Baird, the television pioneer, was born in Helensburgh. John Baird of Kirkintilloch, who died in 1891, constructed New York's elevated railroads on Second and Sixth Avenues.

Balfour

FROM THE LANDS and barony in the parish of Markinch in Fife. Over twenty branches of the family owned land in Fife at one time or another. Close to Milnathort is the ruin of Burleigh Castle, built in the sixteenth century and visited by James VI.

Balfour of Kinloch was one of those who murdered Archbishop Sharp, the episcopalian Archbishop of St Andrews, in 1679.

John Hutton Balfour (1808–84) was a distinguished botanist and Arthur James Balfour (1848–1930) was British Prime Minister, created 1st Earl Balfour of Whittinghame in East Lothian. John Blair Balfour, Lord Advocate for Scotland, 1881–5, was created 1st Baron Kinross of Glasclune in 1902.

Baird

Barclay

THE SCOTTISH and English Barclays are of Norman origin, and the surname derives from Roger de Berkeley who came to England at the time of William the Conqueror and was given the castle of that name in Gloucestershire. Sir Walter Barclay of Gartly, Lord of Redcastle and Inverkeillor, was appointed Chamberlain of Scotland under William the Lion. In later centuries, the Barclays are found in Kincardineshire and Aberdeenshire, but the male line of Gartly ended with Walter, Canon of

Barclay Dress

Barclay Hunting

Moray in 1456. His sister married the Laird of Towie-Barclay and thus the chiefship was carried into that house. The Aberdeenshire Barclays of Tolly had held their estates for over 600 years and their descendant, the Russian Field Marshal Michael Andreas Barclay, was Minister of War at the time of Napoleon's invasion and his defeat in 1812. For this service, he was created Prince Barclay de Tolly.

Beaton

ASSOCIATED WITH the practice of medicine in the Isles in the sixteenth and seventeenth centuries, official physicians to the chiefs of the Macdonalds, and to the MacLaines of Dowart. Martin Martin related that a Dr Beaton was sitting on the upper deck of the *Florida* of the Spanish Armada when it blew up in Tobermory Bay in 1588.

The Beatons of Skye were connected with the Lairds of Balfour in Fife. Dr John Beaton was physician to James VI. James Beaton who died in 1539 was Archbishop of Glasgow and St Andrews, and Regent during the minority of James V. His nephew David became Cardinal and Archbishop of St Andrews who persecuted the Reformers and was murdered in St Andrews Castle. His nephew James was the last Roman Catholic archbishop of St Andrews and ambassador for Scotland in Paris. These latter Beatons descended from the Bethune family who had lands in Fife and Angus and originated from France in the twelfth century.

Bisset

WHEN WILLIAM THE LION returned to his kingdom in 1174, he brought with him 'young Englishmen of good family to seek their fortunes at the Scottish court'. Among these were the 'Biseys'.

John Byset received grants of lands in the north. At a tournament held at Haddington in 1242. Walter Byset, Lord of Aboyne, was worsted by the young Earl of Atholl. In revenge he set fire to the

54

Borthwick Castle, Midlothian

house in which the Earl slept and was consequently banished from the kingdom with his nephew, his lands devolving on other members of the family. Nevertheless, a blood feud seems to have developed with the Atholls.

The Bissets of Lessendrum were among the oldest established families in Aberdeenshire.

Borthwick

THE NAME is believed to be of Celtic origin and is held by a prominent Border family. A Borthwick is recorded as having accompanied the Princess Margaret Aetheling from England to Scotland in 1061; another rescued his Scottish host from the Saracens and recaptured the heart of Robert the Bruce.

In 1357, William de Borthwick received a charter to Ligerwood, near Lauder, and he later acquired land in Midlothian, which he named Borthwick.

The 9th Lord Borthwick was a loyal supporter of Mary, Queen of Scots, providing shelter for her and the Earl of Bothwell at his castle after their wedding. The 11th Lord was the last Royalist to stand out against Cromwell's invasion of Scotland.

Borthwick

55

Borthwick

In 1986 Major John Henry Stuart Borthwick of Crookston, Midlothian, was recognized by the Lyon Court as the 23rd Lord Borthwick.

Boswell

THE NAME is first recorded in Scotland during the reign of William the Lion: one Robert de Boseuille, whose ancestors are believed to have lived in Normandy. In the twelfth century, the family was located in Berwickshire.

James Boswell, the biographer of Dr Samuel Johnson, was born in 1740 in Edinburgh, where his father, Lord Auchinleck, was a Court of Session judge. By then, the family estate lay beside the

*James Boswell
from a portrait by
George Willison*

56

Dean Castle, Kilmarnock, c. *1820*

River Lugar in Ayrshire, and the ruins of two keeps can still be seen. The second is said to have been built by the Boswells in 1612.

By the time James Boswell was a young man, his father was having the third house built, designed by the Adam family. This magnificent mansion is known in the district as 'Affleck Big Hoose'. The old Barony Kirk on the estate houses a Boswell Museum.

Boyd

THE FIRST recorded Boyds were vassals of the De Morevilles in the regality of Largs, and possibly came with them from England. There is a suggestion that the surname might have originated from the island of Bute, which in Gaelic is Bhoid, or Bod.

Sir Iain Moncreiffe of that Ilk suggests a different origin. Walter and Simon, sons of Alan, Hereditary Steward of Dol in Brittany, who came to England in the reign of King Henry I, travelled north to seek their fortune. Robert, Simon's son, became known as Buidhe, the Gaelic name for yellow, which was the colour of his hair. His family were well established in Ayrshire before the reign of King Robert the Bruce, having been granted their lands after the battle of Largs in 1263.

The Lordship of Boyd was created in 1454. Thomas Boyd was created Earl of Arran in 1467,

Boyd

Kelburn Castle, Fairlie, Ayrshire

but the title was later forfeited. William, 10th Lord Boyd, was created Earl of Kilmarnock in 1661.

Dean Castle, Kilmarnock, was forfeited to the Crown after the Boyds had supported Prince Charles Edward at Culloden, but later recovered. The estate was sold to the Earl of Glencairn around 1750, who in turn sold it to Major-General Henry Scott, whose granddaughter married Lord Howard de Walden. In 1975, that family gifted the estate to the town of Kilmarnock.

Boyle

THE FAMILY of De Boyville came from Normandy with William the Conqueror, and a Welsh branch were ancestors of the Earls of Cork and Shannon. Hugo de Morville, a cousin of the De Boyvilles, came to Scotland at the invitation of David I and was appointed Hereditary Great Constable. About 1140, the king made over the lands of Kelvin to the De Boyvilles, but in 1196 the male line died out and the lands passed through a daughter to the powerful earldom of Galloway. This particular male line itself failed in 1234.

The Boyle family have held lands at Kelburn since the reign of Alexander III, and the family seat is still Kelburn Castle at Fairlie in Ayrshire.

The earldom of Glasgow was created for David, Lord Boyle, in 1703. A lawyer, he was ennobled for his work in the preparation of the Act of Union, which joined Scotland with England in terms of government in 1707.

Brodie

THE BRODIES are one of the original Pictish tribes of Moray, and the name comes from the ancient Thaneage. It is known that Michael, Thane of Brodie, received a charter from King Robert Bruce shortly before the battle of Bannockburn, but factual history on the clan is scarce since in 1645 all records were destroyed when Brodie Castle, near Forres, was burned by Lord Lewis Gordon in the Covenanting conflict.

The original castle had been erected in 1609 and the present building, which is owned by the National Trust for Scotland, incorporates the old fortalice. The Brodies recovered their standing after the seventeenth century, and although it is not thought that they participated actively in politics, they maintained a considerable standing in their county.

The notorious Deacon William Brodie who lived in Edinburgh in the eighteenth century, respectable by day, a thief by night, is a disreputable connection. He was hanged by a mechanism of his own devising in 1788.

Broun

A FAMILY of this name were owners of estates in Cumberland shortly after the Norman Conquest in 1066. The name, being a derivation of Brown, is very common throughout Scotland.

The Brouns of Colstoun in East Lothian claim descent from the ancient Royal house of France. They also claim descent from George Broun, who in 1543 married Jean Hay, daughter of the 3rd Lord Yester, ancestor of the Marquesses of Tweeddale. The dowry of the lady consisted of the celebrated 'Coulston Pear', which her remote ancestor Hugo de Gifford of Yester, a famous magician, was supposed to have invested with the extraordinary virtue of securing unfailing prosperity for the family who might possess it.

Members of a younger branch of the Coulston family established themselves as merchants in Elsinore (Helsingør) in Denmark. Broun of Hartrie, near Biggar, is believed to have settled there in the fourteenth century.

Bruce

Brodie

Brodie Hunting

THE FAMILY of de Bruis came from Normandy with William the Conqueror in 1066. They received the lands of Skelton in Yorkshire, and through friendship with King David I of Scotland, Robert de Bruis was gifted the Lordship of Annandale in 1124.

Robert, 5th Lord of Annandale, married Isabella of Huntingdon, second daughter of the Earl of Huntingdon and a great-granddaughter of David I. After the death of King Alexander II, Robert, 6th Lord, was nominated as one of the Regents of the Kingdom of Scotland and guardian of Alexander III. In 1290, after the deaths of Alexander III and his granddaughter and heiress, the Maid of Norway, this same Robert claimed the Crown of

Bruce

59

Scotland as nearest heir. King Edward I of England overruled this claim in favour of John Baliol, who was the grandson of the elder daughter of the Earl of Huntingdon. This Bruce died in 1295 aged 85, and his son married Margaret, Countess of Carrick. Their son asserted the claim again, the throne having fallen vacant through Baliol's renunciation. He ascended the throne of Scotland in 1306, but it was a long, hard struggle before he finally consolidated his position at the battle of Bannockburn, 1314. He died at Cardross in 1329. His remains are interred at the Abbey Church of Dunfermline, although his heart, having been carried to the Crusades, is buried at Melrose Abbey.

King Robert I's only son, David II, died childless, and the Royal line was taken up by the Stewart descendants of Lady Marjorie Bruce. From the Bruces of Clackmannan, cousins of King Robert I, descend the Earls of Elgin, a title conferred in 1633 on Thomas, 3rd Lord of Kinloss.

Edward Bruce, younger brother of King Robert I, went to Ireland in 1315 and was crowned king there in 1316, but was killed in 1318.

James Bruce (1730–94), son of David Bruce of Kinnaird, travelled up the Nile to Abyssinia and in 1790 wrote an account which was thought so implausible that it was branded as fiction.

Robert Bruce (1554–1631), son of the Laird of Airth, anointed Queen Anne at her Coronation in 1590, and opposed King James VI's extreme religious policies.

Sir William Bruce of Kinross (1630–1710) was architect for the restoration of Holyrood Palace (1671–8); designed part of Hopetoun House and built Kinross House.

Thomas Bruce, 7th Earl of Elgin and Kincardine, was a noted archaeologist and brought the Elgin Marbles to England from Greece in 1816. James, 8th Earl, was Governor-General of Canada, 1847–54, and appointed Viceroy of India in 1861.

Although Broomhall is the current home of the Elgin family, there are several locations connected

ABOVE *Robert Bruce's statue, Stirling Castle*

with their history. Most significant perhaps is the Castle of Lochmaben, ancient fortress of the Bruces of Annandale. It is here that the patriot king is believed to have been born.

The tower of the Bruces of Clackmannan can be seen at Clackmannan, south-east of Alloa.

Buchan

THE BUCHANS are an individual clan, although they are associated with the Clan Comyn or Cumming. They are identified as being the old 'Tribe of the Land', as their district once extended from the River Don to the River Deveron. This Highland province was ruled by the Pictish Mormaers of Buchan, who subsequently emerged as the Earls of Buchan in the twelfth century. This was, in fact, the most powerful ancient earldom in the Highlands, and consequently much fought over.

The most famous Buchan of this century was John, 1st Baron Tweedsmuir, the celebrated novelist who was a Member of Parliament and subsequently Governor-General of Canada.

The Buchan Chief holds the barony of Auchmacoy, which is near Ellon in Aberdeenshire.

Buchanan

A STIRLINGSHIRE CLAN of Pictish origin whose lands were on the east side of Loch Lomond. They are said to have descended from an Irishman called Anselan O'Kyan who settled in the Lennox in the eleventh century. A charter from King Alexander II in the thirteenth century confirmed the ownership of the island in Loch Lomond which is now called Clairinch, but at the time was known as Slughorn after the war cry (or slogan) of the Buchquhananes or Buchanans.

King David II officially recognized the family of Buchquhanane in the fourteenth century and the clan prospered with a number of cadet branches: Arnprior, Auchamar, Carbeth, Drumakill, Leny and Spittal.

ABOVE *John Buchan, 1st Baron Tweedsmuir*

OPPOSITE *Auchmacoy, north of Aberdeen*

Buchanan Old Sett

Buchanan Hunting

Towards the end of the seventeenth century, the house and lands of Buchanan were sold to the Marquess of Montrose, Chief of Clan Graham, after the death of John Buchanan of that Ilk. The clan gradually dispersed throughout the following 200 years, although a charitable society was founded in their name in Glasgow to assist boys of the name in their education. One Buchanan of Ulster Scots descent became the 15th President of the United States of America.

The Buchanan Society is the oldest clan society in Scotland, having registered arms in 1919. In 1939, a wealthy clansman purchased Clairinch for the society and the island is now a nature reserve.

Burnett

ROGER BURNARD was established in lands of Faringdon in the thirteenth century. Patrick Burnard held lands in Berwickshire in 1250 and Alexander Burnard or Burnett went north in the train of Robert I and received charters of lands in the forest of Drum and the barony of Tulliboyll in the sheriffdom of Kincardine. The Burnets of Barns, who gave their name to Burnetland in the parish of Broughton, claimed descent from Robertius de Burneville in the reign of David I. Muchalls Castle, near Stonehaven, was built in 1619–27 by the Burnetts of Leys. Crathes Castle on the north of the River Dee in Aberdeenshire was begun in 1553 but not finished until 1594. In the main hall can be seen the Horn of Leys, a jewelled ivory horn said to have been presented to Alexander Burnett by

Robert Bruce in 1323 as a formal token of tenure for his lands. In 1951 the property was taken over by the National Trust for Scotland.

Cameron

THE CLAN NAME is said to derive from the Gaelic *cam-shron*, which means 'crooked nose' or 'crooked hill'; the latter is considered to be the more likely explanation by, for example, Sir Iain Moncreiffe of that Ilk. There were three main branches: the MacSorleys of Glen Nevis, the MacMartins of Letterfinlay and the MacGillonies of Strone, and they inhabited the lands of Lochaber lying on the west side of the loch and the River Lochy, acknowledging the superiority of the Lord of the Isles.

Donald Dubh, progenitor of the Camerons of Locheil, is believed to have led the clan on the side of the Lord of the Isles at Harlaw in 1411. The Camerons of Erracht are said to descend from a marriage between a MacMartin of Letterfinlay heiress and a member of Clan Cameron.

Through all the struggles with the English, the Camerons staunchly supported the Stuart cause. In 1715, Sir Ewen Cameron of Locheil made over

Burnet(t) of Leys Dress

his estates to his grandson Donald enabling his son to muster the clan, for which he was eventually driven into exile. But Donald, known as the 'gentle Locheil', was so impressed by Prince Charles Edward when he invaded in 1745, that he decided that he too would bring out the clan.

In 1793, Cameron of Erracht raised the 79th Highlanders – later to become the Queen's Own Cameron Highlanders.

Cameron lands included Glen Loy and Loch Arkaig, Glen Kingie, Glen Dessary, Glen Pean and Glen Mallie – the lands of Locheil confirmed to an earlier Ewen Cameron by King James IV after the fall of the Lords of the Isles early in the sixteenth century. The clan seat, Achnacarry, stands beside the original castle burned by the Duke of Cumberland in 1746.

Campbell

TRADITION ALLOCATES the origin of this powerful clan to marriage between Eva O'Duibhne, heiress of Clan Duibhne of Lochawe, and the first recorded Campbell in the thirteenth century. Certainly, Sir Colin Campbell of Lochawe was recognized by the King of Scots in 1292 as one of the principal barons of Argyll. The name Campbell itself is derived from the Gaelic *cam-beul* meaning 'crooked mouth'.

Sir Colin's son Neil was a staunch supporter of Robert Bruce, and it is through this relationship that the fortunes of the Campbells came to prosper. For his services, Sir Neil was awarded extensive grants of land including Dunstaffnage, confiscated from the MacDougalls of Lorn. The Campbells of Strachur claim descent from Sir Colin's brother, and from his younger son sprang the Campbells of Loudon. From Sir Neil's younger son came the Campbells of Inverawe.

The Campbells of Glenorchy (Breadalbane) are descendants of Black Colin of Glenorchy, 2nd son of Sir Duncan of Lochow, 1st Lord Campbell, by his wife Lady Marjory Stewart. With the dispersal of the MacGregors from Glenorchy, Sir Duncan gifted the lands to his son, who built the castle of Kilchurn. Through marriage to a co-heiress of John, Lord of Lorn, he acquired one-third of the lands of Lorn.

Cameron of Lochiel

Cameron Hunting

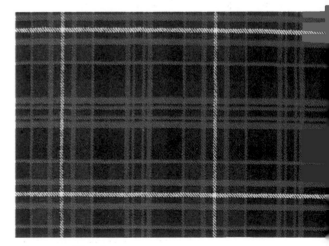

Cameron of Erracht

Campbell of Loudon

Campbell of Argyll Ancient

Campbell of Glenlyon was involved in the massacre of the MacIain MacDonalds of Glencoe, although his chief, Breadalbane, was primarily blamed.

The Campbells of Argyll, the Chiefly House, rose to play prominent roles in the history of Scotland. As the power of the MacDonald Lords of the Isles declined, the Campbells benefited. Argyll acquired Knapdale and Kintyre, and the last great acquisition of land took place in the seventeenth century when Mull, Morvern, Coll and Tiree came into their possession. The titles in the grant of 1701, by which the Earl of Argyll was created Duke, reflect clan territory at its greatest extent: 'Duke of Argyll, Marquess of Kintyre and Lorn, ·Earl Campbell and Cowal, Viscount Lochow and Glenlya, Lord Inveraray, Mull, Morvern and Tiree'. Dukes of Argyll were appointed Heritable Sheriffs of Argyll and Masters of the Household in Scotland, Admirals of the Western Coasts and Isles of Scotland, and keepers of the castles of Dunstaffnage, Tarbert and Dunoon, the first being held under the dukedom by a hereditary captain.

Archibald, 8th Earl, was created Marquis of Argyll in 1641. Known as 'Gillespie Gruamach' or 'Cross-eyed Archibald', he led the more radical Covenanters against King Charles I, but came to an agreement with Charles II, whom he crowned in 1651. His allegiance to Cromwell, however, led to his execution after the Restoration. The forfeited Argyll estates were restored to his son Archibald, but he also backed the wrong horse and was in turn beheaded for his part in the Monmouth Rebellion. The Argyll Campbells proved a resilient breed, and the 10th Earl rose to become 1st Duke in 1701. John, 2nd Duke, was an architect of the Union and was created Duke of Greenwich. He commanded government forces against the Jacobites in 1715 and he was one of the first two Field Marshals ever appointed in the British Army. He dominated Scottish politics in his later years, dying without heir in 1743. He was succeeded as Duke of Argyll by his brother Archibald, who was succeeded by his cousin. John, 9th Duke, born 1845, married Queen Victoria's daughter, Princess Louise, in 1871, but on his death the title passed to his nephew and then to a cousin.

A large and wealthy clan such as the Campbells had many castles, but Inveraray Castle became the principal seat in the fifteenth century when the 1st Earl moved there from Innischonnell Castle,

In 1681, the 11th Campbell of Glenorchy was created Earl of Breadalbane. It was he whom William of Orange entrusted to bring Jacobite chiefs to terms with the revolution, although he was known to have taken a rather non-committal attitude. By this stage, however, the Earl could ride from the east end of Loch Tay to the coast of Argyll without leaving Campbell land. In 1831, John, 4th Earl, was created Marquess of Breadalbane, but with the death of the 2nd Marquess the title became extinct. However, Gavin, 7th Earl, was created Marquis of Breadalbane in 1885, although he too died without issue and thus the marquisate expired. The principal seat of this branch was Taymouth Castle, and there are many cadets of this house.

Barcaldine Castle, Argyll

Castle Gloom

situated on an islet in Loch Awe. The old castle of Inveraray was demolished when the present castle was built in 1773 and there was extensive remodelling after a fire in 1877. The extensive damage caused by another fire in 1975 has been impressively restored. Inveraray Castle in its beautiful setting on the banks of Loch Fyne is still the home of the Duke and Duchess of Argyll.

Cawdor Castle, near Nairn, Morayshire, dates back to 1372 and is the seat of the Earl of Cawdor. Castle Campbell, near Dollar, was built by the 1st Earl of Argyll in the fifteenth century. It was known as Castle Gloom, and burned by Cromwell in the 1650s.

Kilchurn Castle, Loch Awe, Argyll, can be viewed from the outside. The keep was built in

Campbell Breadalbane

Campbell of Cawdor

1440 by Sir Colin Campbell of Glenorchy, founder of the Breadalbane family. Barcaldine Castle, north of Benderloch, was built for 'Black Duncan' Campbell of Glenorchy in 1601.

Colin Campbell of Glenure, known as 'the Red Fox', was murdered on his way to evict tenants of Jacobite chiefs in 1752. The crime became known as the Appin Murder and James Stewart of the Glens was found guilty and hanged for it, although locally it was believed that it was the work of Stewart of Ballachulish.

Sir Colin Campbell, Lord Clyde (1792–1863), commanded the Highland Brigade at Alma and Balaclava. He became a Field Marshal in 1862.

John McLeod Campbell (1800–72) was Minister at Rhu, Dunbartonshire, but was deposed for his views by the General Assembly in 1831. He wrote *The Nature of Atonement*.

Sir Henry Campbell-Bannerman (1836–1908) was the son of Sir James Campbell, a Glasgow draper who became Lord Provost. He took the name of Bannerman in order to benefit from his uncle's will. As leader of the Liberal Party, he became Prime Minister in 1905.

Carmichael

FROM THE BARONY of that name in Lanarkshire. Robert de Carmitely in 1250 had right of lordship in the land of Cleghorn. Sir John de Carmychell had lands of Carmychell in the fourteenth century from William, Earl of Douglas.

John Carmichael became Bishop of Orleans in recognition of the great

OPPOSITE *Cawdor Castle, near Nairn, Morayshire*
BELOW *Inveraray Castle*

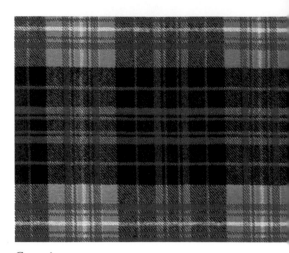

Carmichael   Carnegie

services rendered in France by the Scots. He is known in French history as Jean de St Michel, and in 1429 he founded in his cathedral church a *Messe écossaise* for his countrymen slain at Verneuil.

In Holland the name occurs in the rather eccentric form Carmiggelt, borne by a popular humorous writer.

Carnegie

THE NAME derives from the lands of 'Carryneggy' in south-east Angus, confirmed on John de Ballinhard in 1358 by King David II. The direct line of these Carnegies of that Ilk expired in 1563.

The style of Carnegie of that Ilk was restored by the Carnegies of Kinnaird, near Brechin, at the end of the sixteenth century when they acquired the original family lands. From Duthac de Carnegie, 2nd son of John de Ballinhard, derive the House of Southesk and the House of Ethie.

Sir David Carnegie was created Earl of Southesk by Charles I in 1633 and although the title and estates were forfeited after the Carnegies supported the Old Pretender in 1715, they were later recovered. The earldom of Northesk was assumed by John, younger brother of the 1st Earl of Southesk, who had also previously inherited the earldom of Ethie.

Probably the best-known Carnegie in recent history is the multi-millionaire philanthropist Andrew Carnegie, born the son of a poor weaver in Dunfermline, Fife, in 1835. The family emigrated to Pittsburg in the United States in 1848 and through sheer hard work and determination, Carnegie became at one point the richest man in the world.

In 1897 he bought the estate of Skibo in Sutherland and bestowed considerable gifts on Dunfermline where there is a Memorial Museum. He died in 1918.

Cathcart

OF TERRITORIAL ORIGIN, from the lands of Cathcart in Renfrewshire. The first of the Scottish family came north with Walter Fitz Alan, the first of the Stewards or Stewarts. His name was Rainald, which indicates that he was probably of Breton origin. Sir Alan Cathcart was Warden of the West Marches and was created Baron in 1447. Charles, 8th Baron, was appointed Commander-in-Chief of the British forces in America in 1740, but died on the passage out. His son, William Schaw, became a general and was ambassador to St Petersburg. He was created 1st Earl of Cathcart in 1814.

OPPOSITE *Andrew Carnegie, the steel tycoon who was born in Dunfermline in 1835*

Gosford House, Aberlady, East Lothian

Charteris

THE LANDS of Kinfauns near Kinnoul Hill were given by King Robert Bruce to Thomas de Longueville, who founded the Charteris family. The lands later passed to the Carnegies and then to the Blairs. The ruins of Elcho Castle are located on the south side of the River Tay.

John Wemyss was created 1st Earl of Wemyss in 1633 and his son David constructed the harbour of Methil in Fife. Francis, 2nd son of the 5th Earl, succeeded to the estates and the peerage when his elder brother, Lord Elcho, was attainted for his part in the 1745 Rising. Francis took the name and arms of Charteris of Amisfield under entail from his maternal grandfather, and the Wemyss estates and arms devolved to the 3rd son of the 5th Earl as James Wemyss of Wemyss. Amisfield House, by Haddington, was pulled down after the First World War and the family seat is now Gosford House, Aberlady, East Lothian. Through marriage with the Douglas family, the family acquired the earldom of March and the lands of Neidpath and others in Peebles-shire.

Chattan (Tribal Federation)

THE NAME of this Clan, or Tribal Federation as it became, derives from Gillichattan Mór, the 'Great Servant of St Catan' of the ancient Culdee Church, who lived on the island of Bute. By the twelfth century, the descendants of the saint's family and followers had spread to Glenloy and Loch Arkaig in Lochaber.

In the seventh generation, Eva, an only child, married in 1291 Angus, 6th Chief of Mackintosh. They were compelled to flee from Lochaber for safety and settled in Rothiemurchus where the Mackintoshes had already been established for 150 years. From this time dates the emergence of the great Clan Chattan confederation.

In time the principal branches of Clan Mackintosh (Farquharson of Invercauld, Shaw of Tordarroch, MacThomas of Finegand) were joined by other clans seeking protection (MacBains of Kinchyle, Cattanachs, Macphails, Macleans of Dochgarroch, Gows, Clarks, MacQueens, Macintyres, MacGillivrays of Dunmaglass).

For nearly five centuries Clan Chattan

remained as a powerful and influential force in the Highlands, holding lands that extended from Inverness to Laggan in the Upper Spey Valley.

Cheyne

OF NORMAN ORIGIN from Quesney, near Coutances, a place name meaning 'oak plantation'. The Scots family is believed to be a branch of the Buckinghamshire family of the same name.

Reginald de Chesne became Chamberlain of Scotland in 1267. His grandson was a signatory of the Ragman Roll in 1320. The line seems to have ended with two heiresses: Mary, who married into the Keiths of Inverugy, and Margaret, who held a charter for half the lands of Caithness.

Sir William Watson Cheyne of Leagarth, Fetlar and North Yell, was Lord-Lieutenant of Orkney and Shetland, 1919–30.

Chisholm

NAME FOUND IN Roxburghshire and originally De Chesholm. The original Border seat was the barony of Chisholme. The Highland and the Lowland Chisholms descend from a common ancestor as one of the family married Margaret, Lady of Erchless, daughter and heiress of Wyland of the Aird, and he became Constable of Urquhart Castle on the shores of Loch Ness. His son Thomas, born in 1403, succeeded to his maternal grandfather's lands in Morayshire, and he was forebear of the Chisholms of Comar and Strathglass. Branches of the Highland clan are of Kinneries and Lierty, of Knockfin and of Muckerach.

From the Border family came the Chisholms of Stirches and the Chisholms of Cromlix in Perthshire, three of whom became successive Bishops of Dunblane. The Chisholms supported Prince Charles Edward Stuart in 1745 and many died at Culloden (although two of the Chisholm's sons fought with the Government troops). The Prince took refuge in Strathglass and three of the Seven

Chattan

Chisholm Hunting

Chisholm

75

Cochrane Special

Cochrane

Men of Glenmoriston who protected him are known to have been Chisholms.

The Highland Clearances of the eighteenth and nineteenth centuries drove large numbers of the clan overseas, particularly to Canada, where many of that name are to be found in locations such as Pugwash in Nova Scotia.

Cochrane

NAME TAKEN FROM the lands of Cochrane (Coueran), near Paisley in Renfrewshire. Waldeve de Cochrane witnessed a charter in favour of the 5th Earl of Menteith in 1262. The family was raised to the peerage in 1647 and in 1669 Sir William Cochrane, Baron Cochrane, was created 1st Earl of Dundonald. Archibald, 9th Earl of Dundonald, was a distinguished scientist and inventor. Thomas, 10th Earl (1775–1860), was one of the greatest naval commanders of any age; he conducted an attack on the French fleet at Basque Roads, and, between 1817 and 1828, he commanded the Chilean, Peruvian, Brazilian and Greek navies. He was created Marquess of Maranham in Brazil.

Dundonald, Kyle, a castle built by the Stewarts in the twelfth to thirteenth centuries, was purchased by the Cochranes in the seventeenth century. The Place of Paisley, near Glasgow, was the town house of the Earls of Dundonald after 1653.

Cockburn

THE NAME derives from a location near Duns in Berwickshire. The Cockburns were ancient vassals of the Earls of March and ancestors of the Cockburns of Langton, Ormiston and Clerkington. David II conferred the barony of Carriden in West Lothian on Sir Alexander de Cockburn and Alexander Cockburne was Keeper of the Great Seal of Scotland. Admiral Cockburn conveyed Napoleon to his exile on St Helena.

The Cockburns supported Mary, Queen of Scots, and their castle at Skirling in Midlothian

Cockburn

Bonaly Tower, Colinton, Edinburgh

was demolished in 1568 as a result. Lord Cockburn, the famous nineteenth-century judge and antiquary in Edinburgh's 'Age of Enlightenment', had his home at Bonaly Tower, Colinton, on the outskirts of the capital.

Colquhoun

A TERRITORIAL NAME from the barony of Colquhoun in Dunbartonshire. The founder of the family was Humphrey de Kilpatrick or Kirkpatrick, who obtained a grant of lands in the reign of Alexander II. The lands of Luss were acquired in the fourteenth century by marriage to the 'Fair Maid of Luss', a descendant of Maldwin, Dean of the Lennox in 1150.

In 1603, during the chiefship of Alexander Colquhoun, 17th of Luss, Clan Gregor attacked Luss and then at the battle of Glenfruin, the 'Glen of Sorrow', a further massacre took place. James VI outlawed Clan Gregor as a result and the MacGregor chief was caught through Campbell treachery and hanged with eleven of his principal clansmen.

Colquhoun

77

Colquhoun

Sir John, 19th of Luss, was a necromancer and the last known person openly to practise witchcraft in Scotland. He became one of the first Nova Scotia Baronets and married the Marquis of Montrose's sister, subsequently falling in love and eloping with another of Montrose's sisters. Ross-dhu House, attributed to Robert Adam, was completed in 1773, close to the fifteenth-century castle, now a ruin.

John Caldwell Calhoun, 1782–1850, was Vice-President of the United States of America. A Lieutenant Jimmy Calhoun of the 7th US Cavalry fell fighting the Sioux Indians in Custer's last stand at the battle of Little Bighorn.

Colville

THE NAME is believed to originate from the town of Coleville in Normandy. Philip de Coleuille is recorded in Scotland in the twelfth century, and had the baronies of Oxnam and Heiton in Roxburghshire, having been a hostage for William the Lion under the Treaty of Falaise in 1174.

Sir James Colville received a charter of the Abbey of Culross in 1589 and was created Lord Colville of Culross in 1604. Charles John, 10th Baron and 1st Viscount, was Lord Chamberlain to Queen Alexandra, 1873–1903. David Colville, 1st Baron Clydesmuir, of Braidwood in Lanarkshire, was Secretary of State for Scotland, 1938–40, and Governor of Bombay, 1943–8.

Comyn, Cumming

DESCENDED FROM a Norman noble, Richard Cumyn, the family became powerful in Scotland and in the reign of Alexander III they held the earldoms of Atholl, Menteith and Buchan. By marriage to the sister of King John Baliol, and by descent from King Duncan, John, Lord of Badenoch – the 'Red' Comyn – had a strong claim to the Scottish throne. After a confrontation with Robert Bruce in Dumfries where the Red Comyn was killed, the family went into decline.

The Comyns of Altyre became the chiefs.

Balvenie Castle, Dufftown; Deer Abbey, near Peterhead; the thirteenth-century Inverlochy Castle at Fort William (not the modern castle); the

Comyn, Cumming

Comyn, Cumming Hunting

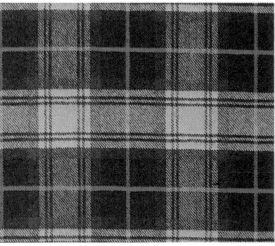

Cranston   Crawford

castle of Lochindorb; and Cruggleton Castle, Garlieston, a massive thirteenth-century fortalice, were all built by members of the Comyn family.

Cranstoun

THIS FAMILY descends from Elfric de Cranston, a Norman who lived in the twelfth century. The Cranstons owned land in Edinburgh and Roxburghshire, and family tombs can be found in Melrose Abbey. The lordship was created in 1609. It became extinct with the death of the 11th Lord Cranstoun in 1813.

Crawford

FROM THE BARONY of Crawford in the upper ward of Clydesdale. In 1248, Sir John of that Ilk died leaving two daughters, of whom the elder married Archibald de Douglas, and the younger married David Lindsay of Wauchopedale, ancestor of the Earls of Crawford and Balcarres. A cadet branch produced Sir Archibald Crawford of Loudoun, the Sheriff of Ayr, murdered at a banquet by the English, and his sister married Sir Malcolm Wallace of Elderslie and was mother to Sir William Wallace, Scotland's great patriot.

Loudoun estates on the River Irvine were originally owned by the Crawfords, but passed through marriage to the Campbells.

The name is found in Sweden as Crafoord.

Crichton

FROM THE OLD BARONY in Midlothian. Turstan de Crectune is recorded in Scotland in 1128. Sir Robert Crichton was created Baron of Sanquhar and Cumnock in 1488. Sir William Crichton, who owned Crichton Castle, was Chancellor to James II. William, 7th Baron, was created Lord of Sanquhar, Viscount of Air, in 1622 and Earl of Dumfries in 1633. Through marriage, the earldom eventually passed to the Marquesses of Bute.

Cumming *see* Comyn

Cunningham

THIS FAMILY descends from Warnibald, who settled in the district of Cunningham, Ayrshire, in the twelfth century. Harvey de Cunningham received the lands of Kilmaurs from Alexander III after the battle of Largs. Alexander de Cunningham was created 1st Earl of Glencairn by

Cunningham

James III in 1488 and was later killed at the battle of Sauchieburn.

Maxwellton House, Moniaive, famous as the birthplace of Robert Burns' Annie Laurie, incorporates part of the fifteenth-century stronghold of the Earls of Glencairn. Kerelaw Castle, at Stevenston in Ayrshire, belonged also to the Glencairn earls, but was sacked by the Montgomeries of Eglinton in the fifteenth century.

The 8th Earl of Glencairn supported Charles II in 1653, but with the death of John, 15th Earl, the title became dormant. The family seems to have become widespread throughout Scotland. The name also appears in France and the Scottish clan are connected with the Irish Conynghams.

Dalrymple

THE FAMILY held a charter for lands in the fourteenth century. James Dalrymple, a Lord of Session as Lord Stair, was created a Baronet in 1664, and later appointed President of the Court of Session. He was created Viscount Stair after the revolution in which King James VII and II was replaced by Queen Mary and William of Orange. His son was the notorious Master of Stair, later 1st Earl of Stair, who issued the letters of 'fire and sword' which led to the massacre of MacIan Macdonalds in Glencoe.

The Dalrymples of Newhailes, Midlothian, descended through Sir Charles Dalrymple-Fergusson of Kilkerran in Ayrshire, and Sir David Dalrymple, Lord Hailes.

Dalzeil

THE BARONY of Dalzell in Lanarkshire is the origin to this name. A kinsman of King Kenneth II, so it is said, was hanged and the king offered a great reward to the man who could rescue the body. A man stepped forward and exclaimed 'Dal Zell', which in old Scots means 'I dare'. The family held lands in Lanarkshire and Dumfries-shire, and a cadet branch built the House of the Binns in West Lothian.

Sir Thomas Dalyell of the Binns (1599–1685) raised the Royal Scots Greys Regiment in 1681 – now the Royal Scots Dragoon Guards. At Rullion Green, Carnethy Hill, beyond Flotterstone Bridge, he won a battle against the Covenanters in 1666. Although legend has it that his body was taken by the Devil, his tomb can be seen at Abercorn Church on the Hopetoun Estate, near South Queensferry. The House of the Binns is currently owned by the National Trust for Scotland.

Dalzeil

Oxenfoord Castle, Midlothian, home of the Dalrymple family, now a school for girls

Davidson

DONALD DUBH of Invernahavon, Chief of the Davidsons, married a daughter of Angus, 6th Mackintosh of Mackintosh, and sought protection from William, 7th of Mackintosh, before 1350, thus becoming associated with the Clan Chattan Confederation. The clan became known as Clan Dhai.

The Davidsons maintained a consistent feud with the Macphersons regarding precedence within Clan Chattan. The famous battle of the Clans fought on the North Inch in Perth in 1396 is believed by some to have been between the Davidsons (Clan Dhai or Kay) and the Macphersons in an attempt to settle their differences.

The main families were the Davidsons of Cantray in Inverness-shire and the Davidsons of Tulloch in Ross-shire. The Chief of Clan Davidson was Hereditary Keeper of Dingwall Castle. The chiefly family of Samieston is recorded as becoming extinct in 1670.

It is interesting to note that a distribution of cloth 'of divers colours' was made by one Walter

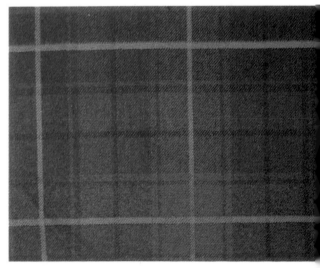

Davidson

81

Douglas

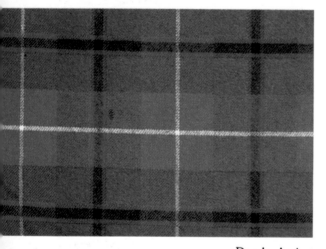

Douglas Ancient

Douglas Grey

Davidson and his men by command of the king in 1429.

Donnachaidh *see* Robertson

Douglas

THE FIRST RECORDED of this name is William de Douglas, who lived in the twelfth century. Grants of land were made to Sir James Douglas, one of Robert Bruce's chief lieutenants. At one time they became the most powerful family in Scotland, and because of their strength and wealth were a constant threat to the Stewart kings. This was the main reason for their title and estates being forfeited in 1455. These Douglases, however, were the ancestors of the earls of Morton, Douglas, Annandale, Moray, Ormond, Angus and Forfar and the dukes of Touraine, Queensberry and Buccleuch and Hamilton.

Lady Margaret Douglas was the daughter of the Earl of Angus and Princess Margaret Tudor, who had been married previously to James IV of Scotland. She married the Earl of Lennox and their son, Lord Darnley, married Mary, Queen of Scots, and was father to James VI and I.

Archibald, 3rd Marquis, was created Duke of Douglas in 1703 but, dying without issue in 1774, his marquisate and the earldom of Angus devolved on the Duke of Hamilton, while the Douglas estates, as a result of the celebrated 'Douglas Cause' lawsuit, passed to his nephew and heir of line, Archibald Stewart, Douglas of Douglas, to whom the armorial bearings and the Douglas chiefship were awarded by Lyon Decree 1771; he was created Lord Douglas of Douglas 1790. On the death of the 4th Lord Douglas in 1857, the estates devolved upon his niece, Lady Elizabeth Douglas of Douglas, Countess of Home, whose great-grandson, Lord Home of the Hirsel, became feudal Baron of Douglas.

Sir Thomas Innes concluded that it was difficult to say who was chief of the name and family of Douglas, and the situation has not changed to date. The arms and estate are merged with the earldom of Home; and the Duke of Hamilton, although paternally a Douglas, became by marriage with the Hamilton heiress, on taking her

*Lady Margaret
Douglas*

name and arms, by the law and custom of Scotland, chief of the name and house of Hamilton (although this is not strictly acknowledged while he carries the family name of Douglas-Hamilton, Lyon not recognizing compound surnames).

Sir Thomas indicates that if Douglasdale were eventually settled, with the name and arms of Douglas, upon a younger grandson of Lord Home, he would thereupon as next of blood bearing the name be Chief of the House of Douglas; failing which that position might pass to the next brother of the House of Hamilton resuming the name and arms of Douglas of Douglas.

The lands of Drumlanrig, near Thornhill in

Dumfries-shire, were confirmed on the Douglases in 1412 by King James I. Douglas of Drumlanrig rose to become Duke of Queensberry, but on the death of the 3rd Duke, the title passed to the Earls of March, and in 1810 to the Dukes of Buccleuch. Threave Castle in Dumfries-shire was built in the fourteenth century for Archibald the Grim, Lord of Galloway and 3rd Earl of Douglas. Aberdour Castle in Fife was owned by the Earls of Morton; Tantallon Castle, near North Berwick, the most impregnable castle in Scotland, was held by the Douglas Earls of Angus. It was taken by Cromwell's General Monck in 1651 after twelve days of continual bombardment. Bothwell Castle, Uddington, was held by the Douglases from 1362 to 1859, and Loch Leven Castle, where Mary, Queen of Scots, was imprisoned, was the property of Sir William Douglas of Loch Leven.

Drummond

THE SURNAME derives from the lands of Drummond or Drymen in Stirlingshire. Malcolm Beg, Steward of the earldom of Strathearn in 1255, is the first recorded and his son, Sir Malcolm, took the name of Drummond. Margaret Drummond married King David II in 1364, and Annabella Drummond married King Robert III.

The lordship was created in 1488. The 4th Lord was created Earl of Perth in 1605. The younger brother of the 3rd Lord Drummond was created Lord Madderty, and from him descend the Viscounts of Strathallan.

The Drummonds supported the Stuarts and followed the fortunes of James VII and II who created them Dukes of Perth and Dukes of Melfort. Both lines became extinct and succession passed to the House of Strathallan. The old Drummond estate passed through an heiress to the Earls of Ancaster.

Drummond Castle is 3½ miles south of Crieff, but the old building of 1491 was destroyed by the Jacobite Duchess of Perth in 1745. Megginch Castle, Carse of Gowrie, and Stobhall, north of Perth, are both Drummond houses.

OPPOSITE *Drummond Castle*

Drummond

Drummond of Perth

Dunbar

CRINAN THE THANE and Seneschal of the Isles was father of King Duncan I and of Maldred, whose son, Gospatric, became Earl of Northumbria in 1067. In 1072, he was deprived of that earldom by William the Conqueror, and coming to Scotland for refuge, was given the earldom of Dunbar by King Malcolm III.

Gospatric's descendant, Patrick, 8th Earl, was also Earl of March. The 9th Earl married Agnes,

ABOVE *Dunbar Castle, East Lothian*

OPPOSITE *Dundas Castle, near South Queensferry*

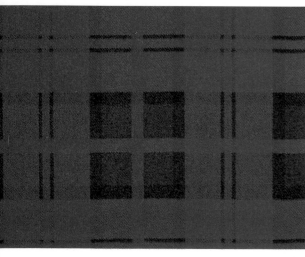

Dunbar

daughter of Thomas Randolph, 1st Earl of Moray, and she is renowned for her spirited defence of Dunbar Castle in 1338. On the death without issue of her two brothers, Thomas, 2nd Earl of Moray, and John, 3rd Earl of Moray, the estate and dignities were enjoyed by Agnes and her sister

Isabella jointly. John Dunbar, the second son of Isabella and her husband, Sir Patrick Dunbar, was created Earl of Moray in 1372 and the elder son, George Dunbar, 10th Earl of Dunbar, succeeded his cousin Patrick, 9th Earl of Dunbar. John Dunbar, Earl of Moray, married Marjorie, daughter of King Robert II.

The Dunbars of Caithness who appear in the fifteenth century are believed to be descended from the Dunbars of Westfield. Sir Alexander Dunbar of Westfield was certainly appointed as Heritable Sheriff of Moray in that century and two of his sons married the co-heiresses of Dunbar of Mochrum and of Cumnock. Eventually there were six baronetcies held by the family: Baldoon and Mochrum in Wigtownshire; Durn in Banffshire; Hempriggs in Caithness; Boath in Nairn; and Northfield in Morayshire. The poet William Dunbar (1460–1520) is believed to have been born near Dunbar in East Lothian.

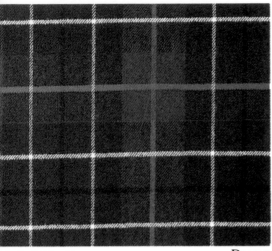

Duncan

Duncans possessed lands in Forfarshire including the barony of Lundie and the estate of Gourdie.

Adam Duncan of Lundie became an admiral and was responsible for the defeat of the Dutch navy off Camperdown in 1797. His son was created Viscount Duncan of Camperdown.

Dundas

SERLE DE DUNDAS is recorded in the reign of William the Lion. The lands of Dundas were obtained by charter from Waldeve, son of Gospatric, most probably in the reign of Malcolm IV. They were undoubtedly a great Lowland family who played a prominent part in the legal affairs of the nation from the time of Sir James, 1st Lord Arniston, who lived in the seventeenth century.

The statesman Henry Dundas, 1st Viscount Melville, was known as the 'uncrowned king of Scotland'. He 'managed' Scotland for William Pitt and he was President of the Board of Control for India. Through his influence many Scots found

Duncan

DESCENDED FROM the ancient Earls of Atholl, the name was taken from a chief of Clan Donnachaidh, 'Fat Duncan', who led the clan at Bannockburn. The Robertson appellation derived from their chief, Robert, in the time of James I. Considered as a sept of Clan Donnachaidh, the

*Henry Dundas,
1st Viscount Melville,
from a portrait in
the National Galleries
of Scotland*

lucrative opportunities in that country. Through his offices many estates forfeited after the 1745 Rebellion were restored, and the ban on the wearing of tartan was lifted.

Arniston House at Gorebridge is owned by the family to this day. Melville Castle, north-east of Lasswade, was built by James Playfair (father of the distinguished William Henry Playfair) on the site of a previous castle and became the home of the 1st Viscount Melville, having passed to him through marriage. Dundas Castle, near South Queensferry, was built by James Dundas of that Ilk in 1424.

In the fifteenth century the Dundas family garrisoned Inchgarvie, an island in the Firth of Forth. The Dundas family of Virginia are descended from a member of the family who emigrated in 1757.

Dundas

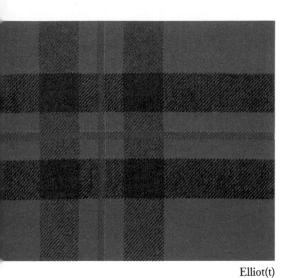

Elliot(t)

Elphinstone

THE VILLAGE of Elphinstone is next to Tranent in East Lothian. Alexander, grandson of Sir Henry Elphinstone of Pittendriech in Midlothian, was created Baron Elphinstone (peerage of Scotland) in 1509 and fell at Flodden Field in 1513. His son fell at the Battle of Pinkie in 1547 and Alexander, 4th Baron, became Lord Treasurer of Scotland. John, 13th Baron, was Governor of Madras, and then of Bombay during the 1857 Mutiny, and was created a United Kingdom Baron.

On his death, this barony became extinct and the Scottish title passed to a cousin, and then to another kinsman who became a Lord–in–Waiting to Queen Victoria. He was created a United Kingdom peer in 1885.

The 16th Baron married Lady Mary Bowes Lyon, a sister of HM Queen Elizabeth the Queen Mother.

Elliot(t)

A FAMILY of southern Scotland, one of the great 'riding' clans of the Borders. The Elliots of Redheugh were recognized as the principal family; one fell at Flodden and one became Captain of Hermitage Castle near Langholm. There was a feud between the Elliots and the Pringles, and at one time it was taken to the Privy Council.

James VI took positive steps to curtail the lawless Border clans and there were executions and banishments. The lands of the Elliots of Redheugh passed to the Eliotts of Stobs, who took over the chiefship.

Gilbert Elliot, who descended from a branch of the Stobs family, and had been under forfeiture in 1685 as an accessory to the rebellion of 1679, received a knighthood, then a baronetcy, having become a Lord of Session as Lord Minto. His son, Sir Gilbert, also became a Lord of Session. The 3rd Baronet, Sir Gilbert, became Lord of the Admiralty and Keeper of the Signet in Scotland. The 4th Baronet, also Sir Gilbert, became Viceroy of Corsica and Governor-General of Bengal, 1807–13. He was created Baron Minto, Viscount Melgund and 1st Earl of Minto.

The 4th Earl was Governor-General of Canada (1898–1904) and Viceroy and Governor-General of Canada (1905–10).

Erskine

THE NAME derives from the barony of Erskine in Renfrewshire and was held by Henry de Erskine in the reign of Alexander II. Sir Thomas de Erskine married Janet Keith, granddaughter of Lady Eline de Mar, and their son, Robert, became heir to one of the oldest Celtic earldoms and Chief of the ancient 'Tribe of the Land' of Mar.

A Mormaer of Mar fought at the battle of Clontarf in 1014. Gratney of Mar married Christian, sister of Robert Bruce, and their son, Donald, was Regent of Scotland. Donald's son, was Great Chamberlain of Scotland. In 1457, before an Assise of Error, the earldom was found to have devolved upon the Crown. Robert, 4th Lord Erskine, was killed at the battle of Flodden and his son, James, 5th Lord, was father of the Regent Erskine.

In 1565, John, 6th Lord Erskine, was restored as Earl of Mar by Mary, Queen of Scots, who was

ABOVE *Braemar Castle, Aberdeenshire*

OPPOSITE *Dirleton Castle, East Lothian*

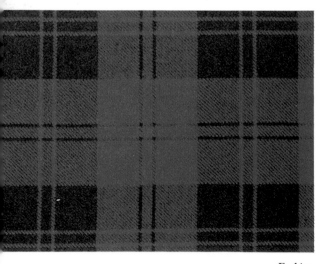

also held to have created a new earldom of Mar. This has caused much confusion since the mid-eighteenth century. The ancient earldom of Mar is the premier earldom of Scotland. The second earldom of Mar, created in 1565, through marriage, acquired the earldom of Kellie in 1835, and the holder of these titles is recognized as the Chief of the clan. In 1715, John Erskine, 6th and 23rd Earl of Mar, led the Jacobite Rebellion and was attainted and his estates forfeited. His estates, however, were purchased by his brother, Lord Grange, and David Erskine of Dun. The Alloa properties were entailed on the heirs male of his daughter, Lady Frances Erskine, who was married to her cousin, James Erskine, Lord Grange's son. In 1824, the earldom was restored. Another Jacobite Erskine, Sir Alexander Erskine of Cambo, Lord Lyon King of Arms, also took part in the 1715 Rebellion, and was imprisoned. By the Restitution of Mar Act 1885, the ancient earldom was claimed by one family, the second earldom was retained by a cousin.

Erskine

Alloa Tower was the fourteenth-century stronghold of the Earls of Mar and, at times, the childhood home of Mary, Queen of Scots. Kellie Castle, near Pittenweem in Fife, was acquired by Thomas Erskine, 1st Earl of Kellie, who was responsible for killing Alexander Ruthven in Perth in the so-called Gowrie conspiracy of 1600. Braemar Castle in Aberdeenshire was built by John, Earl of Mar, in 1628 with the purpose of dominating his vassals, the Farquharson. Dirleton Castle, East Lothian, was owned by Sir John Erskine of Gogar in the seventeenth century.

Farquharson   Fergusson

Farquharson

FARQUHAR, SON OF Alexander Ciar, 3rd Shaw of Rothiemurchus in Strathspey, was originator of this clan, and came to Braemar before the end of the fourteenth century. His son, Donald, married Isobel Stewart, heiress of Invercauld, and he was appointed keeper of the king's forests of Braemar.

Farquhar's son, Finlay Mor, 1st Farquharson of Invercauld, was killed at the battle of Pinkie in 1547. He is said to have been buried in Inveresk churchyard, not far from the battlefield, and the spot was called 'the long Highlandman's grave'.

From Donald there descended a number of cadet families: Inverey, Finzean, Monaltrie and Balmoral. Many of the Farquharsons fought for the Jacobite cause within and outside the Clan Chattan Confederation. Inverey supported the Old Pretender and Invercauld joined the Young Pretender at Perth, although he later went over to the Government, claiming that he had been forced to support the Prince by the Earl of Mar, who was his feudal superior. Invercauld's daughter, Anne, wife of the Mackintosh, restored the clan's honour when she contrived to scatter the English troops with a few of her father's men and thus enabled Prince Charles Edward to escape.

Henry Farquharson, who died in the eighteenth century, was founder of the school of navigation in Moscow, Russia.

Fergusson

THE FIRST SETTLEMENT of this clan would appear to have been at Kintyre. Kilkerran, the seat of the Fergusson chiefs in Ayrshire, is the modern Gaelic form of the name Campbeltown, and is named after St Ciaran, one of the twelve apostles of Ireland, who landed at Dalruadhain in the sixth century.

The Fergussons of Kilkerran descend from Fergus, son of Fergus, in the time of Robert Bruce. Fergus, King of Galloway, in the reign of David I, married a daughter of Henry I of England. The Fergussons of Craigdarroch in Dumfriesshire have a recorded history that dates back to a charter from David II in the fourteenth century.

Other Fergussons lived in Atholl and their Chief was Fergusson of Dunfallandy, and this family can be traced back to the fifteenth century.

The poet Robert Fergusson, who was much admired by his young contemporary Robert Burns, presented a copy of his verses to Kilkerran, his Chief. One of the most distinguished soldiers of this century was Sir Bernard Fergusson, 1st Lord Ballantrae, Governor-General of New Zealand, 1962–7.

Fleming

ORIGINALLY INDICAT-
ING someone from Fland-
ers, the name first appears
in Scotland in the twelfth
century. A family of that
name acquired territories
in Lanarkshire and resided
at Boghall, near Biggar.
Baldwin the Fleming was
Sheriff of Lanark, and
Jordan Fleming was taken
prisoner by the English
with William the Lion in 1174.

Sir Sandford Fleming from Kirkcaldy (1827–
1915) was chief engineer of the Canadian Pacific
Railway and author of Standard Time. Sir Alexander Fleming (1881–1955), the discoverer of
penicillin, was born at Darvel, near Kilmarnock.

Fletcher

THIS NAME means 'arrow maker' and is therefore
found all over Scotland. The Fletchers followed
the clans for whom they made arrows. In Argyll
they are associated with the Stewarts and
Campbells; in Perthshire with the Macgregors. In
the sixteenth century, the Fletchers entered into a
bond with Campbell of Glenorchy and possessed
Achallader in Glen Tulla for several generations.
Branches of the family held baronies at Inver-
peffer and Saltoun, in East Lothian.

Andrew Fletcher of Saltoun (1653–1716) was a
Member of Parliament who bitterly opposed the
Duke of Lauderdale and the Duke of York, later
James VII and II, in their plans to devolve power
from Scotland to England. He was exiled, but
returned at the time of William and Mary,
defiantly leading the anti-unionist movement.

Forbes

THE CLAN FORBES is said
to originate from one
Ochonochar, who slew a
bear and won the up until
then uninhabitable Braes
of Forbes in Aberdeen-
shire. His family settled
there and a charter of 1271
altered the tenure to feudal. Alexander de Forbes
was one of the fiercest op-
ponents of King Edward I

of England and lost his life defending the castle of
Urquhart beside Loch Ness. His son died at the
battle of Dupplin in 1332 at which Edward Balliol
and the 'disinherited barons' who opposed Robert
Bruce defeated the Regent Mar.

The first Lord Forbes, created a peer in 1445,
married a granddaughter of Robert II. There
were a large number of cadet branches: Pitsligo,
Boyndlie, Callendar, Castleton, Rothiemay,
Culquhonny, Culloden, Tolquhon, Waterton,
Thainston, Pitnacalder, Foveran, Brux, Led-
macoy, Belnabodach, Kildrummy, Towie,
Invernan, Corsindae, Balfluig, Monymusk,
Leslie, Corse, Craigievar and Echt.

Duncan Forbes of Culloden was Lord
President of the Court of Session at the time of the
1745 Rebellion and used his great influence to
oppose the Prince's cause, but then afterwards
fought valiantly to ease the cruel reprisals inflicted
on the Highlands.

Fletcher   Forbes

The Forbes built and owned many beautiful castles, notably Craigievar in Aberdeenshire, which belongs now to the National Trust for Scotland; Monymusk, a sixteenth-century tower, which had been an Augustinian priory; Pitfichie Castle near Monymusk; and Drumminor, near Rhynnie. Corgarff Castle, Strathdon; Pitsligo Castle and Colquhonnie Castle, Strathdon; and Corse Castle in Aberdeenshire are all ruins.

Forsyth

THE NAME could be from the Gaelic *Fearsithe*, meaning 'man of peace'. Robert de Fauside signed the Ragman Roll in 1296. Later Forsyth chiefs became members of the Royal Stewart household at Falkland and their arms are shown in early sixteenth-century armorials.

In 1980, Alistair William Forsyth, who descends from a Falkland laird living in 1607, was recognized as being of the chiefly line. Supported by a petition representing 2000 Forsyths, a Gilfine of nine elders of the Clan, which by ancient custom may petition the Crown through the Lord Lyon King of Arms, requested recognition of the Chief. After investigation, the petition received

ABOVE *Duncan Forbes of Culloden by J. Davison*
BELOW *Falkland Palace, Fife*

Forsyth · Forsyth Ancient

Lyon's approval and the clan was restored to formal recognition after a period of more than 300 years.

Fotheringham

THE NAME comes from a parish in Inverarity in Angus and is said to be a corruption of Fotheringhay in Northamptonshire, which was held by the royal house of Scotland in the twelfth century as part of the Honour of Huntingdon. The Fotheringhams of Ballindean, Perthshire, descend from the family at Powie in Angus. The latter descend from Henry de Fodringhay who received lands near Dundee from Robert II.

Fraser

THE WORLD-WIDE family of Fraser traces its ancestry to Anjou and Normandy. There is evidence to suggest that they sailed with William the Conqueror in 1066. The main line of Fraser developed from Sir Gilbert of Touch-Fraser, who died in 1263. Sir Laurence Abernethy was created 1st Lord Saltoun in

1445. Through marriage with Alexander Fraser of Philorth, the title and chiefship passed to that family.

Alexander Fraser, 7th of Philorth, built Fraserburgh Harbour in 1546. Sir Alexander, 8th of Philorth, acquired charters from James VI to create a burgh out of the fishing villages of Faithlie and Broadsea. He also intended a university, but his finances became so stretched that he was forced to dispose of the Manor of Philorth. It was recovered in 1661, but in 1915 Philorth House was destroyed by fire. The present Chief, Lady Saltoun, is married to Captain Alexander Ramsay of Mar, a grandson of the 13th Earl of Dalhousie and a great-grandson of Queen Victoria.

Hugh Fraser was one of the hostages for the

Fraser

Fraser Hunting

Gair, Gayre

THE HOUSE OF GAYRE arose in Cornwall before the thirteenth century from the great Domesday manor of Gayre. In time, the senior line became extinct and the second line migrated to Yorkshire and became involved in the destruction of a castle, which forced them to flee to Scotland.

Through marriage to the Mowes of Mowe and, later, to the MacCullochs of Nigg, a branch of the MacCullochs of Plaids, the family settled in the north-east of Scotland (the MacCullochs of Plaids were custodians of the Girth of St Duthac, Tain, a noted medieval shrine venerating the eleventh-century chief confessor of Ireland and Scotland).

The current Chief has declared that the Duthus of the clan is at Minard Castle, Loch Fyne, since the twentieth-century oil-related developments on the ancient lands make that location unsuitable. At Minard Castle are records, a library, a small armoury and a family portrait gallery.

ransom of James I, who created him Baron of Kinnoll, but he is sometimes known as the 1st Lord Lovat. His grandson, Hugh, was created Lord Lovat or Lord Fraser in or around 1460. Simon, 11th Lord Lovat, was outlawed in 1698 for having seized the widow of the 9th Lord, getting the marriage ceremony performed and forcibly consumating the nuptials. He returned in 1715 to support the Government forces and his outlawry was reversed. In 1740, he joined the Young Pretender, who appointed him General of the Highlands and created him Duke of Fraser. He was arrested in 1746 and beheaded on Tower Hill, London. His honours and estate were forfeited, but his eldest son obtained full pardon, subsequently becoming a British general.

The 15th Lord Lovat distinguished himself on the beaches of Normandy with his Lovat Scouts during the Second World War.

Galbraith

THE NAME means 'Briton's son' in Gaelic, and probably they originated from among the Britons who settled in Strathclyde. The clan is connected with the Earls of Lennox through Clan Macfarlane. At one time the Galbraiths took protection from Clan Donald, and they are connected with the island of Gigha.

Thomas Dunlop Galbraith, Minister of State for Scotland, 1955–8, was created 1st Baron Strathclyde in 1955.

Fullerton

FROM THE BARONY in the Dundonald parish in Ayrshire. Alanus de Fowlertoun founded and endowed a convent of Carmelite or White Friars at Irvine. A branch of the family settled in Arran in the fourteenth century. In 1327 Robert I granted the land of Foulertoun in the sheriffdom of Forfar to Galfridus de Foullertoune, with the office of falconer. The family held these lands for over a

Gardyne

FROM THE BARONY of Gardyne in Angus where for many years there was a family of that Ilk. The name is common in the Arbroath area. Gardyne Castle, which is privately owned, is located near Forfar, Angus.

Gair, Gayre

Galbraith

Galbraith Ancient

Gillies

Gillies

A NAME associated with Badenoch and the Hebrides; it means 'servant of Jesus'. In the twelfth century one Uhtred, son of Gilise, held lands in Lothian.

Sir William Gillies, CBE, RA, RSA, RSW (1898–1973), was a distinguished President of the Royal Scottish Academy.

Gordon

THE EARLIEST RECORD of the name Gordon in Scotland was in the late twelfth century and related to the parish of Gordon in the Merse in Berwickshire. Adam de Gordon was an Anglo-Norman, and was with King Louis XI of France in the Crusades in 1270. Under Robert Bruce, Sir Adam, Lord of Gordon, acquired the lordship of Strathbogie in Banffshire. He died at the battle of Halidon Hill in 1333. His great-grandson died at the battle of Homildon in 1402 leaving a daughter, Elizabeth, as heiress. She married Sir Alexander Seton, second son of Sir William Seton of Seton, and their son was created 1st Earl of Huntly in 1449.

For the next century the Gordons held autocratic sway over the Highlands and James IV was a frequent visitor to Huntly Castle, which until 1544

Gordon

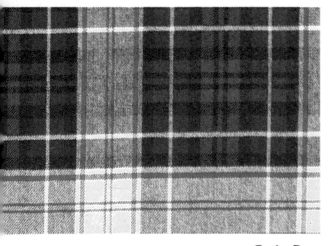

Gordon Dress

ABOVE *Haddo House*

OPPOSITE *Huntly Castle*

had been known as Strathbogie Castle. The 4th Earl had aspirations to marry one of his sons to Mary, Queen of Scots, and through a series of misunderstandings there was a rebellion which brought about the collapse of Gordon power after their defeat at Corrichie.

The 5th Earl also rebelled against James VI in 1594, and much of Huntly Castle was blown up as a result. Three years later, the 5th Earl succeeded in making peace with his monarch and he became 1st Marquess of Huntly.

The dukedom was created in 1684, but in 1836 the 5th Duke died without issue. The nearest heir, George, became 9th Marquess of Huntly and Chief of the name.

The Gordons of Haddo were created Earls of Aberdeen in 1682 and are descended from Patrick Gordon of Methlic, who fell at the battle of Arbroath in 1445. The 4th Earl was British Prime Minister, 1852–5. John, 7th Earl and 1st Marquess of Aberdeen and Temair, was Governor-General of Canada, 1893–8, and Lord Lieutenant of Ireland, 1905–15.

John Gordon of Glenbuchat, known as 'Old Glenbucket' was a staunch Jacobite. Active in the uprisings of 1715 and 1745, he was forced to flee to Norway after Culloden and died abroad.

George Gordon, 6th Lord Byron, the poet, was related to the Gordons of Gight.

Gow or MacGowan

Graham Menteith

Graham Montrose

Gow or MacGowan

GOW IS THE GAELIC *gobha*, meaning 'blacksmith'. The smith was obviously a man of importance, since the clans depended so greatly on horses for their mobility. The name therefore appears connected with many clans, although specifically with the MacPherson in the Clan Chattan Confederation.

The MacGowans are recorded as an old Stirling family. In the reign of David II there was a Clan M'Gowan who lived beside the River Nith in Dumfries-shire. They are connected with a king of the Britons who died in 1018.

Graham

THE FIRST RECORDED Graham appears to be William de Graham, alive in the twelfth century, one of an illustrious Anglo-Norman family. There is a popular belief that the Grahams descend from 'Gramus', who demolished the wall built by the Roman Emperor Antoninus between the Firth of Clyde and the Firth of Forth, but this has been completely dismissed by a number of notable historians.

William de Graham received the lands of Abercorn and Dalkeith from David I. His descendants acquired the lordships of Kinnabar and Old Montrose in 1325, and Sir William Graham married Mary, second daughter of Robert III. Patrick, their eldest grandson, became Lord Graham, then 1st Earl of Montrose in 1504. James, 5th Earl, was the celebrated 1st Marquis who supported Charles I and Charles II against the Commonwealth. He was a brilliant military leader and wrote some remarkable poetry. James, 4th Marquis, was created 1st Duke of Montrose, and played a significant part in the restoration of tartan.

Another member of the clan was John of Claverhouse, Viscount Dundee, 'Bonnie Dundee', the persecutor of the Covenanters and staunch Jacobite campaigner, who died a hero at the battle of Killiecrankie fighting against the English troops of William of Orange in 1689.

Old Claverhouse Castle, Dundee, was the birthplace of John Graham of Claverhouse and the spot where the castle stood is marked by a dovecot.

James Graham, 1st Marquis of Montrose, 1649

Braco Castle in Perthshire was a seat of the Grahams of Braco in the seventeenth century. Kincardine Castle, near Auchterarder, was the seat of the Graham Earls of Strathearn, but passed to the Grahams of Montrose. The original castle was dismantled by the Marquis of Argyll in 1645. Brodick Castle on the Isle of Arran passed to the Montrose family through marriage with the daughter of the 12th Duke of Hamilton.

Grant

A MAIN BRANCH of the 'Siol Alpine' of which Clan Gregor is chief. The originator of the Grants is said to have been Gregor Mor MacGregor, who lived in the twelfth century in Strathspey. Sir Lawrence Grant, Sheriff of Inverness in 1263, is the first recorded ancestor, although it is believed that the family may have originated from Nottinghamshire, where their lands adjoined those of the Bissets,

101

Grant

into which family they had married and who came north in the service of Henry III of England.

The Grants of Freuchie were given a knighthood by James VI and I. In 1704, Sir Humphrey Colquhoun, 5th Baronet of Luss, obtained a new patent with original precedence giving remainder of his title to his son-in-law, James Grant, who subsequently became 6th Baronet. Through the marriage of Sir Ludovic Grant, 7th Baronet and 20th Chief of the name, to Lady Margaret Ogilvie, daughter of the Earl of Findlater, the earldom of Seafield was later acquired by the 9th Baronet. The 7th Earl was created Baron Strathspey in 1884, and when the 11th Earl died in 1915, the earldom devolved upon his only daughter and his brother succeeded to the Strathspey title and also the chiefship.

Gray

HUGO DE GRAY is recorded in Scotland in the thirteenth century and his family are believed to have come from Normandy. The surname is now common all over Scotland, but in 1377 the lands of Fowlis passed to the Gray family through marriage to a daughter of the Maule family, who had received

them for military services from David I. Huntly Castle at Longforgan, now incorporated into an industrial school building, was built in 1452 for Lord Gray of Fowlis, Master of the Household to James II.

At one time the title passed into the earldom of Moray.

Francis, 14th Baron, who died in 1842, was Postmaster-General for Scotland.

Grierson

THE GRIERSONS of Lag, Dumfries-shire, descend from Gilbert, second son of Malcolm, Dominus de MacGregor, who lived in the fourteenth century. Gilbert Grierson had a charter of lands in the Stewartry of Kircudbright from Princess Margaret, daughter of Robert III, and widow of the 4th Earl of Douglas.

Gunn

BELIEVED TO BE DESCENDED from Gunni, the grandson of Sweyn Asleifsson, the 'Ultimate Viking' who was killed in Dublin in 1171.

A warlike clan who occupied the northern areas of Caithness and Sutherland, they were sworn enemies of the Keiths and in 1426, at Harpsdale,

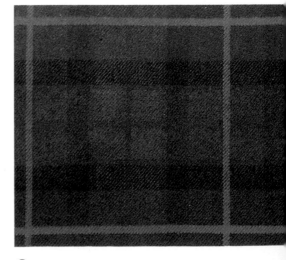

Gunn

south of Thurso, a particularly bloody, but nevertheless indecisive, battle took place. Although the Gunn chiefs once held splendid court at their castle of Clyth, 2 miles east of Lybster, they were listed as one of the 'broken clans' of the north in 1594. At the time of the Highland Clearances in Sutherland, many clansfolk emigrated to New Zealand and Canada, where they founded a new Kildonan.

There is a Clan Gunn Museum north of Latheron, not far from Helmsdale.

Guthrie

Guthrie

FROM THE BARONY of the name in Angus, which is near Forfar, although it is also said to derive from Guthrum, a Scandinavian prince. It was Squire Guthrie who brought Sir William Wallace back to Scotland from France in 1299.

Sir David Guthrie was King's Treasurer in the

fifteenth century and built Guthrie Castle, near Friockheim, in 1468. The existing house was built about 1760 and connected to the tower in 1848.

BELOW *Guthrie Castle, near Friockheim, Angus*

Field Marshal Sir Douglas, Earl Haig

Haig

PETRUS DEL HAGE is recorded in the mid-twelfth century. The Haigs have lived at Bemersyde, near Dryburgh in Roxburghshire, since 1162, although the ancient prophecy attributed to Thomas the Rhymer:

Tide, tide, whate'er betide,
There'll aye be Haigs at Bemersyde

was proved untrue in 1867 when the direct line died out and the property was sold.

In 1921, however, Bemersyde was purchased and presented to Field Marshal Sir Douglas, Earl Haig, as a gift from a grateful nation for his work in the First World War. Alexander Haig, who resigned from the Nixon Administration as Secretary of State, is a member of the American branch of the family.

Haldane

THERE ARE TWO suggested origins of this name. The first is that it derives from Old English Healfdene (Old Danish Halfdan) and means 'half Da '. The second theory is that a member of the Border house of Hadden or Howden acquired the estate of Gleneagles, Perthshire, by marrying the heiress. In the thirteenth and fourteenth centuries, the family were recorded as being barons of consequence in Perthshire.

Richard Burdon Haldane (1856–1928) became Lord Chancellor and 1st Viscount Haldane of Cloan, near Auchterarder. Miss Elizabeth Sanderson Haldane (1862–1937) was the first woman Justice of the Peace in Scotland; and the writer, Lady Naomi Mitchison, is a granddaughter of Lord Haldane.

Hamilton

THE CLAN descended from Walter Fitz-Gilbert of Hameldone, noted in 1295, and granted the lands of Cadzow by Robert Bruce. The surname is not thought to derive from Hamilton in Lanarkshire, but possibly from Hambleton in either Yorkshire or Lancashire. The Lord Hamilton who married James II's eldest daughter descended from Walter. The king's grandson became Earl of Arran in 1503, and his grandson was made Marquis of Hamilton in 1599. James, 3rd Marquis, was created Duke of Hamilton in 1643. The title passed to his daughter, Anne, who married William Douglas, Earl of Selkirk, later connecting the dukedom with the Douglas family, although the Duke remains Chief of the Hamiltons, *not* the Douglases.

Branches of the family include the Dukes of Abercorn and the Earls of Haddington. Hamilton House, Prestonpans, was built for Sir John Hamilton, brother of the 1st Earl of Haddington, in 1628.

Sir Thomas Hamilton, President of the Court

Hamilton House, Prestonpans

of Session and Keeper of the Privy Seal, was created Lord Binning in 1613 and 1st Earl of Haddington in 1627. The title devolved in 1858 on to George Baillie through his mother and thus Mellerstain, the magnificent Adam house 8 miles from Kelso, passed to the Baillie-Hamilton family. Lands at Tyningham, near East Linton, were granted to the 1st Earl in 1628 and his descendants built Tyningham House.

In the eighteenth century Lord Blantyre bought Lethington, near Haddington, home of the Maitlands of Lethington, and renamed it Lennoxlove; this is now the seat of the Dukes of Hamilton and Brandon.

The Place of Paisley was owned by the Hamilton family until 1653. The magnificent Hamilton Palace, located in what is now Strathclyde Regional Park, was pulled down in 1922–32

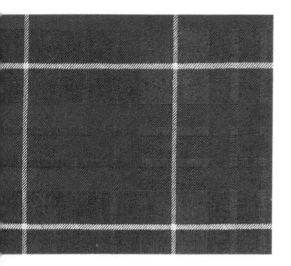

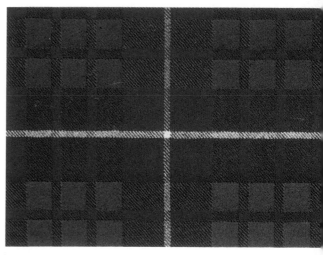

Hamilton Hunting   Hamilton

Mellerstain, Berwickshire

as it was found to be sinking as a result of coalmining operations in the area. There is a mausoleum in the grounds erected to the 10th Duke, who died in 1852. Craignethan Castle, Crossford, was a fifteenth-century Hamilton stronghold which, with Cadzow Castle in Hamilton High Park, was destroyed by the Earl of Moray in reprisal for Hamilton support of Mary, Queen of Scots.

Dalzell House, Motherwell, was the seat of the Hamiltons of Dalzell. They moved to Surrey in 1952 and the property is now owned by Motherwell District Council. Brodick Castle, on the Isle of Arran, may date back to the fourteenth century. It passed to the Duke of Montrose through his marriage to the daughter of the 12th Duke of Hamilton, but was offered to the treasury as payment of death duties and is now owned by the National Trust for Scotland.

Hannay

THIS FAMILY sprang from the ancient province of Galloway. The earliest known possessors of Sorbie Tower were the powerful Anglo-Norman family, the Viponts, Lords of Westmorland, who received the lands and manor in 1185. Records from the thirteenth century are sparse, but it is believed that the change of ownership to the Hannays could have been through marriage, as the family mottos are remarkably similar.

The Hannays supported John Balliol who, through his mother the Lady Devorgilla, represented the old Celtic Lords of Galloway. In 1308, they were forced to submit to Edward Bruce when he conquered Galloway. A Gilbert de Hannethes signed the Ragman Roll in 1296.

The Hannays rose to Sauchieburn and Flodden; they feuded against and sided with their neighbours, the Kennedys, the Dunbars and the Morays, and they joined James IV on his pilgrimages to St Ninian's shrine at Whithorn. In 1601, the Hannays were outlawed for their behaviour towards the Murrays. The Hannays of Kirkdale had their seat between Creetown and Gatehouse-of-Fleet from the sixteenth century. They owned Rusco Castle, near Gatehouse-of-Fleet, from 1786 and Sorbie Tower, 7 miles south of Wigtown, has been restored by the Hannay Society. Kingsmuir estate, near Crail in Fife, is the seat of the Hannays of Kingsmuir.

Hannay

Hay

Hay

THERE ARE TWO accounts concerning the origins of the Hays. The first, traditional, one concerns the battle of Luncarty, believed to have taken place around AD 971. Kenneth III was fighting the Danes and the day was saved by a countryman and his two sons. The king commanded that a falcon be let loose from Kinnoull Hill, and that as far as it flew, the lands would belong to the hero and

his sons. The bird flew to a stone in St Madoes parish, taking in some of the best land in the Carse.

The name Hay, however, is documented as dating from the eighth century in France. La Haya de Puits was a senior leader with William the Conqueror's army, and William de Haya was Pincerna (butler) to William the Lion. William de Haya's son was one of the hostages held in England with William the Lion and on his return, was granted an extensive manor in Erroll. His younger brother, Robert, was progenitor of the Earls of Tweeddale.

Sir Gilbert de la Hay, 3rd Lord of Erroll, co-Regent of Scotland in 1255, married Lady Idonea

Comyn, daughter of William, Earl of Buchan, and sister of the then Lord High Constable of Scotland. Their son, Sir Gilbert, also fought with Robert Bruce and was rewarded with the lands of Slains, near Aberdeen, and the post of Hereditary Lord High Constable of Scotland, a post which the family retains. In 1946, the Countess of Erroll married Sir Iain Moncreiffe of that Ilk.

Their eldest son succeeded to the earldom of Erroll in 1978 and the baronetcy of Moncreiffe in 1985.

The Hays married into the family of Hugo de Gifford and acquired the lands of Yester. John Hay was created Baron Yester of Yester in 1478. John, 8th Baron, was created 1st Earl of Tweeddale in 1646, and the 2nd Earl, who was Lord Chancellor of Scotland in 1704–5, was created 1st Marquess of Tweeddale.

The 1st Baronet of Smithfield and Haystoun, Peebles-shire, was an Esquire of the Body of James VI. Sir Gilbert Hay of Dronlaw, 2nd son of Sir Thomas Hay or Erroll, is the ancestor of the Hays of Park, Wigtownshire. Smithfield, Haystoun and Park are all Nova Scotia baronets.

Duns Castle in Berwickshire was built in the fourteenth century for Randolph, Earl of Moray, but the estate came to the Hays of Drumelzier in the seventeenth century. Neidpath Castle, near Peebles, was a Hay stronghold but passed to the family of the Earl of Wemyss. Slains Castles in Aberdeenshire (Old and New) are ruins now, but Dr Johnson and James Boswell stayed at New Slains on their tour of Scotland.

Yester Castle, near Gifford, erected in 1268 by Hugo de Gifford, ancestor of the Hays of Yester, is located near the magnificent Yester House, built by the Adam family of architects, but sold by the widow of the 11th Marquess of Tweeddale for tax

ABOVE *Duns Castle,
Berwickshire*

OPPOSITE *The remains
of Old Slains Castle,
north of Aberdeen.
The timber-framed house
behind is owned by the
current chief*

RIGHT *John, 1st Marquis
of Tweeddale, by
Sir Peter Lely*

reasons. At Delgattie Castle, Turriff, there is a Clan Hay centre and Leith Hall, home of the Leith-Hays, is owned by the National Trust for Scotland.

Henderson or MacKendrick

EANNIG MOR MAC RIGH NEACHTAN, Big Henry, son of King Nectan who ruled Caledonia in the eighth century AD, is claimed as the founder of this name, although one researcher on the subject declares that this idea is 'preposterous'. King Nectan was the forebear of the MacNaughtons and built the Pictish tower of Abernethy.

The Henderson held lands encompassing Glencoe, Argyll, and were hereditary pipers to Clan Abrach. The direct line is believed to have terminated with an heiress, and through marriage the Hendersons became part of the Macdonald

Henderson

Hepburn

Clan Ian of Glencoe. Their last chief, therefore, was killed at the massacre of Glencoe in 1692.

The chief Lowland family of the name resided at Fordel Castle, near Inverkeithing in Fife. They are believed to have descended from the old Dumfries-shire family of Henryson. William Henrison was chamberlain of Lochmaben Castle in the fourteenth century.

Hepburn

FROM HEBBURN in the parish of Chillingham, in Northumberland. The family appears around 1271. Adam de Hepburne is said to have been taken prisoner by the Earl of March, who later gave him lands in East Lothian for saving his life when he was attacked by a savage horse. In the sixteenth century there were Hepburns of Hailes, Waughton, Bolton, Beanston, Humbie, Keith, Nunraw, Monkrigg, Smeaton and Alderston. Bothwell Castle, near Uddingston in Lanarkshire, was bestowed upon Patrick Hepburn, Lord Hailes, but later exchanged for the barony of Hermitage in Liddesdale.

Nunraw Abbey was founded as a convent in c. 1158 and became in the sixteenth century the preserve and then, after three Hepburn prioresses, the residence of the Hepburn family. In 1548, the Scottish parliament met here to decide on sending the child Mary, Queens of Scots, to France.

James Hepburn, 4th Earl of Bothwell

Fordel Castle, Fife

James Hepburn, 4th Earl of Bothwell (1536–78), was a powerful and turbulent noble who escorted Mary, Queens of Scots, back to Scotland from France. Having played a part in the murder of Mary's husband, Lord Darnley, he later married the Queen. At Carberry Hill, Bothwell offered to fight any of Mary's enemies single-handed, but was forbidden to by the Queen. In 1570, Mary was granted a divorce and in the meantime, Bothwell had fled to Scandinavia where the Danish king held him in solitary confinement in Dragsholm Castle, where he died insane.

Home

ALDAN DE HOME derived his name from the lands of Home in Berwickshire in the twelfth century. His descendant, Sir Thomas, married Nichola, the heiress of Dunglass. Sir Alexander Home was Ambassador to England in 1459 and created Lord Home in 1473. Alexander, 6th Lord Home, was created 1st Earl of Home in 1605. Charles, 12th Earl, was ADC to Queen Victoria, 1887–97. Through marriage to the heiress of the Douglas fortunes, the family acquired the lands of Douglas, Bothwell and others in Angus. There has been a dispute concerning the chiefship of Douglas, but it is stated by the Lyon Court that the Chief of Home cannot also be Chief of Douglas. The 11th Earl, however, Keeper of the Great Seal of Scotland, was created Baron Douglas in 1875.

David Hume, the eighteenth-century philosopher and historian, spelled his name with a 'u', whereas his brother insisted on spelling his with an 'o'.

The Hirsel at Coldstream in Berwickshire is the seat of the Earls of Home. In 1963, the 14th Earl renounced his title in order to become British Prime Minister, being returned later to the House of Lords as Lord Home of the Hirsel.

Fast Castle, Coldingham, was built for the Homes in the thirteenth century, and Hume Castle, south of Greenlaw, was once the family seat.

Lord Home of the Hirsel

Hope

JOHN HOPE of Peebles-shire is recorded in the thirteenth century. The Earls of Hopetoun are descended from John de Hope, one of the retinue of Queen Magdalen, wife of James V.

Sir Thomas Hope was created 1st Baronet in 1628. His grandson, Sir Charles, was created 1st Earl of Hopetoun in 1703. James, 3rd Earl, succeeded to the estates of his grand-uncle, the 3rd Marquess of Annandale, in 1792.

John, 7th Earl, was Governor of Australia, 1900–2, and created 1st Marquess of Linlithgow. The 2nd Marquess was Viceroy and Governor of India, 1936–43. Thomas Hope of Craighall in Fife was created a Baronet of Nova Scotia in 1628. Luffness House, Aberlady, East Lothian, built in the sixteenth century on the site of a Norse camp, is the home of the Hopes of Luffness. Hopetoun House, South Queensferry, home of the Marquesses of Linlithgow, is considered one of Robert Adam's masterpieces.

OPPOSITE *Hopetoun House, South Queensferry*

Home

Hunter of Hunterston   Hunter

Hunter

A FAMILY who came to Scotland about 1110 from Normandy. Aylmer le Hunter of the County of Are signed the Ragman Roll in 1296. The lands of Hunter were granted to William Hunter by Robert II in 1374. The ancient castle of Hunterston stands in the grounds of the abandoned Hunterston House; the lands around have been acquired by the Atomic Energy Authority. The chiefship passed to the Cochrane-Patrick family who have changed their name to Hunter of Hunterston.

Hunter's Quay, Dunoon, is named after the Hunters of Hafton House, who in the mid-nineteenth century bought up this coastline. The Hunterian Museum, University of Glasgow, houses the art collection built up by the physician William Hunter (1718–83).

Cadet families are Hunter of Polmood, Bonnytoun and Doonholm, Auchterarder and Thurston, and Hunter-Blair of Blairquhan.

Irvine

Innes

Baronet, succeeded as 5th Duke of Roxburgh in 1805. Innes of Balvenie was created Baronet in 1628. Sir Alexander Innes of Coxton in the County of Moray, from a younger branch of the Innermarkie family, was created Baronet in 1686.

Sir Thomas Innes of Learney was Lord Lyon King of Arms, 1945–69. His younger son, Malcolm Innes of Edingight, became Lord Lyon in 1981.

Irvine

A TERRITORIAL surname from Irving, an old parish in Dumfries-shire, and from Irvine in Ayrshire. Robert de Hirewine appears in the thirteenth century, and William de Irwyne obtained the Forest of Drum in 1324 from Robert I, and is thus the ancestor of the Irvines of Drum.

Jardine

DU JARDIN was a name recorded at the battle of Hastings, and it is assumed that the family settled in the vicinity of Kendal in the twelfth century and then moved to Lanarkshire – the Wandel and Hartside area – in the thirteenth century. It was early in the fourteenth century when they settled in Dumfries-shire, where they have been ever since.

Innes

ORIGINATED IN Moray in 1160 in the reign of Malcolm IV, when the lands of Innes in the district of Elgin were given to Berowald, a man of Flanders. John Innes was Bishop of Moray and rebuilt Elgin Cathedral after it had been burned by Alexander Stewart, the Wolf of Badenoch.

Robert Innes, 19th Feudal Baron of Innes, was created a Baronet in 1625. Sir James, 3rd Baronet, married Lady Margaret Ker, daughter of Harry, son of the 1st Earl of Roxburgh. Sir James, 6th

Johnston(e) Ancient

Johnston(e)

The Chiefly House is Jardine of Applegirth, a Nova Scotia baronetcy created in 1672. The Buchanan-Jardines of Castle Milk in Dumfriesshire descend from the founders of Jardine Matheson & Co, the famous Hong Kong-based Merchant Trading company. The 2nd Baronet assumed the additional surname of Buchanan.

Johnston[e]

A POWERFUL Border clan, they held the central area of Annandale, and Sir James of that Ilk became 1st Earl of Hartfell in 1643. The legend is that the Chief of the Johnstons, while at the Scottish court, heard of the English king's planned treachery to dispose of Bruce in favour of Baliol and sent Bruce a spur with a feather tied to it to indicate 'flight with speed'. Bruce acted on the hint and later rewarded the Johnston accordingly.

The Johnstons of Caskieben, Aberdeenshire, and of Westerhall, Dumfries, are both Nova Scotia baronetcies.

The Johnstones were intermittently appointed Wardens of the West March, alternating in that role with the Maxwells, with whom they had a deadly feud, which they resolved in 1623. The 2nd Earl of Hartfell became Marquess of Annandale in 1701.

The Aberdeenshire Johnstons claim descent from Stiven de Johnston in the fourteenth century. Their seat of Caskieben, Blackburn, was purchased from them by John Keith and is now the seat of the Earls of Kintore.

The Border stronghold was Lochwood Tower, near Beattock, burned by the Maxwells in 1593.

Keith

ONE OF THE MOST powerful Celtic families. The hereditary office of Great Marischal of Scotland was held by them, and for supporting Robert Bruce they received the lands of Kintore. The Keiths were created Earls Marischal in 1458.

The Hon. Sir John Keith, 3rd son of the 6th Earl Marischal, was created 1st Earl of Kintore. The 2nd Earl supported the Old Pretender and lost the office of Knight-Marischal which went to his son, the 3rd Earl, at a later date. The 3rd Earl's brother succeeded. The Earls Marischal had also supported the Old Pretender and that title was attainted in 1715. The Kintore title passed into the Falconer family in 1778.

The town of Peterhead was founded in 1593 by the 5th Earl Marischal. The statue in front of the Town House is of James Keith, brother of the 10th Earl, who became a Marshal in the army of Frederick the Great of Prussia.

Keith Hall at Inverurie, formerly the home of

Keith

OPPOSITE *Devil's Beef Tub, near Moffat, associated with the Johnston family*

ABOVE *Dunottar Castle*

the Johnston family, is the seat of the Earls of Kintore. Dunottar Castle, south of Stonehaven, is built on an ancient fortified site mentioned in the seventh century. The oldest part of the castle was built in the fourteenth century by Sir William Keith. Scotland's Regalia was brought here for safe keeping when Cromwell invaded Scotland. When the castle was besieged, the various items were smuggled out to the nearby church of Kineff. The 5th Earl Marischal had his town mansion in the building that now houses the Bank of Scotland in Marischal Street, Aberdeen.

Kennedy

A Galloway/Ayrshire family, descendants of Duncan of Carrick who lived in the twelfth century. James of Dunure married Mary, daughter of Robert III. Their son, Sir Gilbert, was one of the six Regents of Scotland during the minority of James III. He became 1st Lord Kennedy in 1452. David, 3rd Lord Kennedy, became 1st Earl of Cassilis in 1502 and was killed at the battle of Flodden. Gilbert, 2nd Earl, was assassinated by Sir Hugh Campbell of Loudon, Sheriff of Ayr, and supporter of the Douglas Angus faction, from whom Gilbert had unsuccessfully attempted to rescue James V.

Archibald, 12th Earl, was created 1st Marquess of Ailsa.

Castle Kennedy was built by the Earls of Cassilis in 1607, but passed to the Earls of Stair. Dunure Castle, near Culzean, is where the Earl of Cassilis is said to have roasted the lay abbot of Crossraguel in an attempt to make him surrender abbey lands in 1507.

Culzean Castle, the 'jewel in the crown' of the National Trust for Scotland, was built by Robert Adam for the 10th Earl of Cassilis on the site of an ancient Kennedy castle.

RIGHT *Dunure Castle*

Kennedy

OPPOSITE *Culzean Castle*

ABOVE *Newbattle Abbey*

Kerr

THIS FAMILY originally settled in the Scottish Borders in the fourteenth century. They are believed to have been of Viking descent arriving by way of France where they had first settled. Living in the Borders of Scotland at that time demanded qualities of toughness, courage and wit, and the Kerrs are remembered as being successful Border 'reivers'. Kerr of Cessford was appointed Warden of the Middle March in 1515. Mark Ker, eldest son of Ker of Cessford, Abbot of Newbattle, had the Abbey of Newbattle erected into a temporal lordship in 1587. He was created 1st Earl of Lothian in 1606. Anne, Countess of Lothian, married Sir William Kerr of the Ancram branch of the Kerrs of Ferniehurst: a zealous Covenanter who in 1633 was created Lord Kerr of Nisbet, Longnewton and Dolphinstoun and Earl of Ancram. In 1631, he was created Lord Newbottle and 1st Earl of

Lothian. Robert, 4th Earl, was created 1st Marquess of Lothian in 1701. Schomberg Henry, 9th Marquess, was Secretary for Scotland and Keeper of the Great Seal, 1887–92; Philip Henry, 11th Marquess, was Ambassador Extraordinary to Washington in 1939–40 and is considered the father of European federalism.

Kerr

121

Kerr Ancient

Lamont

Ferniehurst Castle, near Jedburgh in Roxburghshire, is the fifteenth-century stronghold of the Kerrs of Ferniehurst, burned by the Earl of Sussex, but rebuilt in 1598. Monteviot, Jedburgh, is the home of the Marquesses of Lothian in recent years, but Newbattle Abbey, near Edinburgh, is the seventeenth-century mansion gifted by the nation to Phillip, 11th Marquess. It is now a residential college.

Kirkpatrick

SAID TO BE FROM a chapel formerly dedicated to St Patrick in the parish of Closeburn. The first of the name appears to be Roger de Kirkpatrick and his heirs had a charter from Robert Bruce near the Water of Esk. A Roger de Kirkpatrick is said to have been with Robert Bruce when he encountered and stabbed the Red Comyn in the thirteenth-century Franciscan friary. Bruce is supposed to have rushed out saying, 'I doubt I have slain the Comyn', whereupon Kirkpatrick replied, 'I'll mak siccar', and went into the church supposedly to make sure.

Towards the end of the eighteenth century, William Kirkpatrick of Conheath, a wine merchant, married Dona Francesca, daughter of Baron de Grivegnée. One of their daughters married the Count del Montijo, and their daughter, Eugénie, married the Emperor Napoleon III.

Lamont

THE NAME derives from the Old Norse for 'lawman' and the clan is traditionally attributed to Ferchar in the thirteenth century. At one time the family owned the greater part of Cowal but, like the MacDougalls, the Lamonts opposed Robert Bruce and suffered accordingly. John Lamont of that Ilk, however, held a charter from James III and his seat was Toward Castle, 4 miles south of Dunoon.

In the seventeenth century, Sir James Lamont of Inveryne supported the 1st Marquess of Montrose, carrying 'fire and sword' into Campbell country. Both Toward Castle and Ascog Castle, on the Isle of Bute, were destroyed. Both castles surrendered following promises of life and liberty, but the Campbells slaughtered 'the whole gentlemen of the name Lamont'.

Not surprisingly, what remained of the clan scattered. The chiefship passed to a cadet branch which emigrated to Australia. A Clan Lamont Society, however, was formed in 1895. At Dunoon there is a memorial to the murdered Lamonts at Castle Hill.

Lauder

OF NORMAN ORIGIN, de Lavedre is mentioned among the barons at the time of Malcolm Canmore. Sir Robert de Lawedre, a companion in

Bass Rock

arms of Sir William Wallace, was Ambassador to England for Robert I. William Lauder was Bishop of Glasgow and Chancellor of Scotland and his brother was Bishop of Dunkeld in the fifteenth century.

The 2nd Baronet of Fountainhall, Haddingtonshire, was Senator of the College of Justice with the courtesy title of Lord Fountainhall. The 5th Baronet married Isabel Dick, heiress of Grange. The family name was changed to Dick-Lauder. At one time the Lauders owned the Bass Rock, where there is the ruin of a castle.

Sir Harry Lauder, the famous music hall entertainer, was born at No. 3 Bridge Street,

Sir Harry Lauder

Musselburgh. He bought the Glenbranter estate in Argyll, and later had his home at Lauder Ha', Strathaven.

Lennox

ALWIN MACMUREDACH MACMAIDOUERN, Mormaer of the Levanach, is the first Celtic earl of this name and he lived in the twelfth century. The earldom of Lennox was associated with various of the Stewarts. Lord Darnley, for example, who married Mary, Queen of Scots, was son of the 4th Earl of Lennox.

Charles Lennox was the natural son of Charles II by the Duchess of Portsmouth (who was also

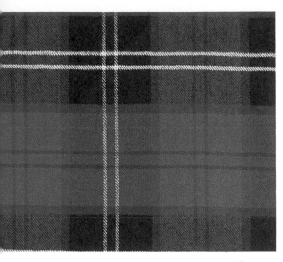

Lennox

Leslie Ancient

created Duchesse d'Aubigny by Louis XIV of France). In 1675 he was created Duke of Richmond.

Charles, 4th Duke, was Governor-General of Canada, 1818–19. Charles Henry, 6th Duke of Richmond and Lennox, Secretary for Scotland and Keeper of the Great Seal, was created Duke of Gordon in 1876.

Lennox Castle, at Lennoxtown in Stirlingshire, is a former seat of the Lennox of Woodhead family.

Leslie

FROM THE BARONY of Lesly in the Garioch. Descent from Bartolf, a Hungarian nobleman who was chamberlain to St Margaret, Queen to Malcolm Canmore, is laid claim to.

By marriage the Leslies acquired the baronies of Rothes, Fytekill and Ballinbriech. George Leslie of Rothes and Fytekill was created 1st Earl of Rothes in 1457, and John, 6th Earl, was created Duke of Rothes in 1680. On his death, the dukedom became extinct, but the earldom continued through the female line.

Sir Alexander Leslie, having served with the Swedish army, in which he attained the rank of Field Marshal in 1638, took command of the Covenanters' army and defeated the king's troops

Leslie

Leslie Red

Edzell Castle

in various engagements. At the treaty of peace signed in 1641, the king created him Lord Balgonie and Earl of Leven. In 1682, through his parent's marriage, the 3rd Earl of Leven acquired the earldom of Melville.

David Leslie, routed by Cromwell in 1650, was created 1st Lord Newark in 1661. Leslie House at Kirkcaldy, built by the Duke of Rothes, was burned down in 1763. Balgonie Castle, Markinch, was constructed in the fifteenth century for Alexander Leslie, Earl of Leven. Pitcarlie House, north of Auchtermuchty, was the home of Patrick Leslie, Lord Lindores, in 1600. Balquhain Castle, Inverurie, a sixteenth-century ruined tower, and Pitcaple Castle near by belonged to the Leslie family.

Lindsay

BALDRIC DE LINDSAY, a Norman, is first recorded. In 1180, William de Lindsay was Baron of Luffness and Laird of Crawford. Walter de Lindesey, who lived in the twelfth century, was succeeded as 2nd Lord Lindsay by his son, William of Ercildun. Sir David, 13th Lord, was created 1st Earl of Crawford and married a daughter of Robert II. He was Ambassador to England. David, son of Lord Menmuir, was

Part of the Livingston memorial at Blantyre; see p. 128

created Lord Lindsay of Balcarres in 1633. His son was created Earl of Balcarres in 1651. Alexander, 6th Earl of Balcarres, Governor of Jamaica, succeeded as 23rd Earl of Crawford in 1808.

The 1st Earl of Crawford's uncle was Sir David Lindsay of the Byres. John, 10th Lord Lindsay of the Byres, was created 1st Earl of Lindsay in 1366.

David, 27th Earl of Crawford and 10th Earl of Balcarres, was Minister of Transport in 1922.

Edzell Castle, Brechin, was acquired by the Crawford Lindsays, who built a new castle in the sixteenth century. They purchased the Balcarres estate in Colinsburgh in 1587.

Livingston

LEVING, A SAXON, held lands in West Lothian in the twelfth century. These lands were called Leving's-toun. Members of this family were prominent in Scottish history between 1300 and 1715. They held several peerages, notably the earldoms of Callendar, Linlithgow and Newburgh. Callendar House at Falkirk

Lindsay   Livingston

Fast Castle

was held by the Livingstons from the fourteenth century. The small Highland clan of Livingston from the Isle of Lismore and Western Argyll originally bore a Gaelic name spelled in different ways – MacDunsleinhe, Mac-an-Leigh, or Maclea – and they were connected with the Stewarts of Appin. There is no known blood tie between the Lowland and Highland families. David Livingstone (1813–73), the famous explorer, although born at Blantyre in Lanarkshire, descended from the Highland clan. There is a national memorial to his memory in Lanark.

Lockhart

ORIGINALLY this family came from England and settled at Lee in Lanarkshire in 1272. Sir Simon Locard carried the key to the casket in which Robert the Bruce's heart was placed for the Crusades. To commemorate, the family name was altered to Lockhart. On the Crusades, Sir Simon acquired the Lee Penny, the original of Sir Walter Scott's *Talisman*.

Barr Castle, Girvan, was a fifteenth-century tower erected by the Lockharts. The lands of Carnwath have been held by the family since the seventeenth century. Fatlips Castle, on Tinto Hill, was a stronghold, although also held by the Turnbulls. The lands of Lee were acquired in the twelfth century and the castle rebuilt in the nineteenth century.

Logan or MacLennan

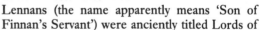

THERE ARE TWO distinct families, one Highland and one Lowland. Of the latter, Sir Robert Logan of Restalrig married a daughter of Robert II and in 1400 he was appointed Admiral of Scotland.

The MacLennans of the north are descended from the Logans of Drumderfit, Easter Ross. The MacLennans (the name apparently means 'Son of Finnan's Servant') were anciently titled Lords of

Loch Erne. In Ossianic poetry, Lide MacLennan and his clan of 1200 men appear. The MacLennans held territories in Lorne, Mull, Tiree and on Iona, but after a defeat at Inverness they retired to Glenshiel, where they have remained for centuries.

Fast Castle, Coldingham, a Home stronghold, passed by marriage to the last Logan of Restalrig in 1580. He died there after being outlawed for his involvement in the Gowrie conspiracy. The lands of Restalrig in Edinburgh were also confiscated at this time.

Lumsden

THE NAME derives from the lands of that name on the coast of Berwickshire, near Coldingham, and it is first mentioned in a charter dated 1098 of Edgar, King of Scots, son of Malcolm Canmore. The earliest recorded owners of the land are Gillen and Cren de Lumisden, who witnessed various charters in 1166, and Adam Lumsden of that Ilk who, together with Roger de Lummesdene, did forced homage to Edward I of England in 1296.

The family acquired the lands of Blanerne, Berwickshire, by charter in 1329, and by the mid-fourteenth century, offshoots had charters to Conlan in Fife and Medlar and Cushnie in Aberdeenshire.

Blanerne or Lumsden Castle, Duns, was acquired in the fourteenth century. Cushnie, Alford; Pitcaple Castle, Inverurie; and Tillycairn Castle, Cluny, are owned by the family.

Logan

Logan or MacLennan

Lyle

A FAMILY of this name were barons of Duchal in Renfrewshire in the thirteenth century. The first of the name in Scotland appears to be Ralph de Insula, a follower of the Steward from Northumberland. In 1296, John del Ille of Berwickshire and Richard del Isle of Edinburghshire did forced homage to Edward I of England. The Duchal Lyles ended in the sixteenth century with an heiress who married Porter of Porterfield.

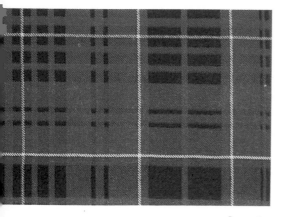

Lumsden

Leonard Lyell, nephew and heir to Sir Charles Lyell, 1st Baronet created 1864, was Member of Parliament for Orkney and Shetland, 1885–1900, and was created 1st Baron Lyell in 1914.

Lyon

THE FIRST of the name recorded in Scotland is Thomas Lyon in the pay of Edward II in the fourteenth century. A John Lyon had a charter of lands of Forteviot and Forgundenny in Perthshire from David II. John Lyon, secretary to David II, had a charter from Robert II of the Thaneage of Glamis as a free barony, and in 1376 he married the king's daughter, Princess Joanna.

The origin of the Lyon family is uncertain. They have been ascribed to the usual Norman descent, though it is possible they were of Celtic origin and a sept of Clan Lamont. Whatever the truth, Sir John founded a line of feudal barons and later earls that still flourishes in the family's red sandstone castle of Glamis.

Sir John was murdered by Sir James Lindsay of Crawford, Scotland's Ambassador to England. His grandson was created a Peer of Parliament in 1445 as Lord Glamis, having been held a hostage for James I by the English.

After the death of John, 6th Lord Glamis, his wife, a Douglas, was accused of witchcraft by James V and was burned alive outside Edinburgh Castle. The castle of Glamis was claimed by the Crown, and it was only after James V's death that the 7th Lord Glamis was restored to his properties. The 9th Lord Glamis was created 1st Earl of Kinghorne by James VI. Patrick, 3rd Earl of Kinghorne, received an addition to his title and became known as the Earl of Strathmore and Kinghorne, as have his successors since.

The 9th Earl married a great Durham heiress, Miss Mary Eleanor Bowes of Streatlam Castle and Gibside, and the 10th Earl, being given the United Kingdom title of Lord Bowes, changed the family name to Bowes Lyon.

In 1923, the 14th Earl's youngest daughter, Lady Elizabeth Bowes Lyon, married Prince Albert, Duke of York, second son of King George V. At the abdication of King Edward VIII, the Duke of York ascended the throne as King George VI with the Duchess as Queen Consort, and ultimately she became HM Queen Elizabeth, the Queen Mother.

MacAllister

A BRANCH OF Clan Donald which traces its origin to a great-grandson of Somerled. Clan lands were in Kintyre and the seat was on the north-west side of West Loch Tarbert. A later seat was Loup, and these lands were held until the early nineteenth century. The clan was numerically strong in Bute and

MacAllister   MacAlpine

Glamis Castle

Arran, and the MacAllisters were Constables of Tarbert Castle, Loch Fyne.

Kennox, west of Stewarton in Ayrshire, was the later seat of the clan acquired by marriage.

Sir Donald MacAllister of Tarbert was Principal, later Chancellor, of Glasgow University.

MacAlpine

SIOL ALPINE is a name that appears in a number of clans with no apparent connection. Considered to be a branch of the royal Clan Alpin, of the Kings of Dalriada. Monaghe fiz Alpyn of the county of Perth rendered forced homage to Edward I of England in 1296. John McAlpyn, prior of the Friar Preachers at Perth and later a reformer, is better known as Machabeus. He died in Copenhagen, 1557.

The baronets of Knott Park in Surrey, founders of the firm of Sir Robert McAlpine & Sons, civil engineers, come from Lanarkshire and the title was bestowed in 1918.

MacAndrew *see* Anderson

MacArthur

ONE OF THE OLDEST of Argyllshire clans, claimed to be the older branch of Clan Campbell. They supported Robert Bruce and were granted extensive lands in Argyll, including those of the MacDougalls who had opposed Bruce. In the middle of the fourteenth century they were at the height of their

MacArthur

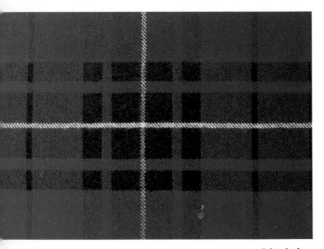

MacAulay

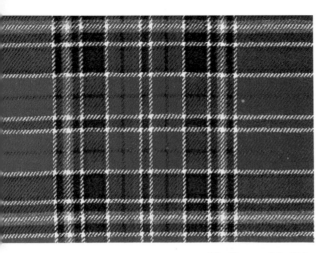

MacBean or MacBain

power and their Chief was appointed Captain of Dunstaffnage Castle. In the fifteenth century, the MacArthur Chief was beheaded by James IV and most of the estates forfeited.

The seat of the clan was Strachur and a sept of the name were hereditary pipers to the Macdonalds of the Isles.

In America, General Arthur MacArthur became Lieutenant-General in 1906, the twelfth officer in the US Army to attain that rank. His son was the equally famous General Douglas MacArthur.

MacAulay

THERE ARE TWO clans of this name. One was a branch of Clan Alpine, and in the sixteenth century entered into an agreement with the MacGregors of Glenstrae. The MacAulays of Lewis were of Norse descent and unconnected with the MacAulays of Ardencaple; they were followers of the MacLeods of Lewis. The name appears in Sutherland and in Ross-shire around Ullapool.

The lands of Ardencaple were retained by the MacAulays until the 12th Chief sold them to the Duke of Argyll in 1767.

MacBean or MacBain

THE MACBEANS are believed to have come from Lochaber and settled in eastern Inverness-shire. Myles MacBean supported Mackintosh against the Red Comyn. The principal family was MacBean of Kinchyle. In 1959 an American, descended from this branch, was acknowledged as Chief by the Lord Lyon King of Arms.

The MacBain Memorial Park at Kinchyle on the south shore of Loch Ness, north of Dores, was created by Hughston MacBain of MacBain, acknowledged as 21st Chief.

MacCallum   MacCallum Red line

MacColl

MacCallum

THE NAME means 'son of the gillie of Calum'. The MacCallums held the lands of Poltalloch. Some time before 1850, the head of the family of Poltalloch changed the name from MacCallum to Malcolm for 'aesthetic reasons'.

John Wingfield Malcolm of Poltalloch was created Lord Malcolm in 1896 and died in 1902.

See also Malcolm.

MacColl

THE MACCOLLS are a branch of the Clan Donald and settled around Loch Fyne, joining in the feud with the MacGregors. Many also settled in the area of Ballachulish in Appin and these followed the Stewart of Appin.

At Kenmore on Loch Fyne there is a monument to Evan McColl (1808–98), the Gaelic poet and author of *The Mountain Minstrel*.

MacCorquodale

A DISTANT SEPT of the MacLeods of Lewis, they held lands on the northern side of Loch Awe, which were granted to Torquil, the forebear of the family, by King Kenneth Mac-Alpine. They had their ancient seat at Loch Tromlee, 2 miles north of Taycreggan.

MacCorquodale

133

MacCulloch

LULACH WAS the King of Scots who succeeded Macbeth, but was promptly dispatched by Malcolm Canmore.

The Highland MacCullochs seem to have owned considerable lands in the province of Ross. MacCullochs in Argyllshire tended to be associated with the Clan MacDougall.

The origin of the Galloway MacCullochs is totally obscure. The name first appears in 1296 when Thomas Maculagh of Wigtown rendered forced homage to Edward 1 of England, and was probably then Sheriff of Wigtown.

Cardoness Castle, Gatehouse-of-Fleet, was a MacCulloch stronghold after 1450, and Barholm Castle, Creetown, was held by them in the sixteenth and seventeenth centuries. Their castle of Myreton at Port William was acquired by the Maxwells of Monreith in 1685.

Clan Donald Centre, Isle of Skye; see p. 138

MacDonald

THE CLAN DONALD is undisputably the largest of all the Highland clans, at one time controlling virtually the whole of Scotland's western seaboard from the Butt of Lewis in the north to the Mull of Kintyre in the south, with possessions in Ireland also, and in the Isle of Man.

According to the claims of certain historians the clan descends from Conn of the Hundred Battles, Ard Righ of Ireland in the first century AD through Colla Uais, the first of the family to settle in the Hebrides, and from whom comes the designation 'Clan Cholla', the Children of Coll.

Somerled, Lord of Argyll in the twelfth century, unable to overcome the Norse invaders, married Ragnhildis, daughter of Olave the Red of Norway. Through marriage and conquest, Somerled acquired power over the isles. After his death, his sons inherited their shares of the islands, and through them descend the MacDougalls of Argyll and Lorn, and Clan Donald, sometimes referred to as the MacDonalds of Islay.

The name of Clan Donald derives from Donald of Islay, grandson of the mighty Somerled. Donald had a number of children, but in particular, two sons, Angus Mor and Alasdair Mor. From the latter descend the Clan Alister, the MacAllisters of Loup. Angus Mor's son, Angus Og, supported Robert Bruce and was granted many of the vast territories formerly possessed by his ancestors.

In 1354, Angus Og's son, John of Islay, took the title of Dominus Insularum, or Lord of the Isles, having married the heiress to Garmoran, the Uists, Benbecula, the Small Isles and half of Lochaber. From his natural son, Iain nan Fraoch, descend the MacDonalds of Glencoe. The eldest son from this marriage to Amy MacRuari was ancestor of the MacDonalds of Clanranald and the MacDonnells of Glengarry. John of Islay later divorced his wife and married Princess Margaret, daughter of Robert II. Their eldest son succeeded as Lord of the Isles; their second son, Iain Mor, 'The Tanister', founded the MacDonalds of Islay and Kintyre; the third son, Alexander or Alister Carrach, founded the house of MacDonald of Keppoch and, by his marriage to Marjorie Bisset of Antrim in Ireland, the MacDonnels of Antrim.

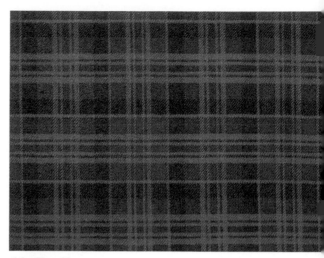

MacDonald

MacDonald Lord of the Isles Hunting

ABOVE *Flora MacDonald, who rescued Prince Charles Edward Stuart*
LEFT *Duntulm Castle, Trotternish, Isle of Skye*

For a time Gaelic culture flourished, there being harmony between the various rulers of the west, tied together by common blood. In 1424, however, Alexander of Harlaw inherited through his mother the earldom of Ross. He was succeeded by his son John, the fourth and last MacDonald of the Isles and, also, Earl of Ross. This chief's inability to govern brought about an inter-family civil war. The Crown intervened and at a naval engagement known as the battle of Bloody Bay, the Lord of the Isles was defeated. The title was forfeited in 1493, since when it has remained with the dukedom of Rothesay and is retained for the eldest son of the reigning British monarch.

The decline of the MacDonald dynasty in the West Highlands runs parallel with the decline of Gaelic culture. Despite attempts by several MacDonald leaders to re-establish the old order, particularly against the rise of Campbell power in their region, by the seventeenth century the various branches – Sleat, Clanranald, Glengarry, Keppoch, Glencoe – had all become individual and independent clans with their own chiefs, none of whom would claim to be Mac Dhomnuill. This was the situation throughout the troublesome

LEFT *James Ramsay MacDonald*

OPPOSITE *Castle Tioram*

times of the seventeenth and eighteenth centuries until the battle of Culloden and the end of the clan system in 1746.

Not until 1947 was Clan Donald again to have a High Chief, when the Lord Lyon King of Arms granted Alexander MacDonald of MacDonald, 7th Lord MacDonald, the undifferenced Arms of MacDonald, Chief of the Name and Arms.

On the island of Skye in the grounds of Armadale Castle, Sleat, is the Clan Donald Centre, which has been financed by members of the clan around the world. There are various ruined castles in the area all originating from Clan Donald, and Flora Macdonald, the heroine of the 1745 Rebellion, who went to live in North Carolina for a period before the American War of Independence.

MacDonald Clanranald

On the island of Islay there are the ruins of Finlaggan, the palatial residence of the Lords of the Isles. Dunnyvaig Castle is the ruined seat of the MacDonalds of Islay and Kintyre. At Glencoe in 1692, Government forces massacred the MacIan MacDonalds as an example to the Highlanders who failed to show allegiance to William and Mary of Orange.

Castle Tioram in Moidart is the ruined stronghold of the MacDonalds of Clanranald. At Glenfinnan, there is a monument raised by Mac-Donald of Glenaladale to the men who fought for Prince Charles Edward Stuart in 1745–6. The ruined Invergarry Castle at Invergarry in Lochaber was the fortress of the MacDonnells of Glengarry.

The story of Clan Donald is the story of the

MacDonald Dress

139

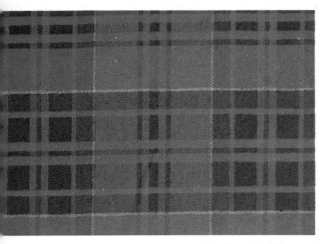

MacDonald of Keppoch

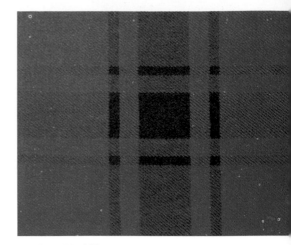

MacDonald of Sleat

MacDonnell of Glengarry

West Highlands of Scotland. Those who are particularly interested are well advised to read MacDonald of Castleton's magnificent work entitled *Clan Donald*.

Many MacDonalds have contributed to the world we live in and, although scattered far and wide, they share a common ancestry. Sir Hector MacDonald (1852–1903) was the hero of the Sudan; Jacques Etienne MacDonald (1765–1840) was made a Marshal of France and created Duke of Taranto; Sir John Alexander MacDonald (1815–91), born in Glasgow, was Prime Minister of Canada; James Ramsay MacDonald (1866–1937), British Prime Minister this century, was born in Lossiemouth.

MacDonnell *see* MacDonald

MacDougall

DOUGLAS OR DUGALD, son of Somerled, is ancestor of this clan. Unfortunately for the Mac-Dougalls, their chief supported the losing side in the contest between Robert Bruce and the Comyns, and was deprived of his lands. At the time the family controlled Lorn and Benderloch, the islands of Mull, Lismore, Coll and Tiree, with castles like Dunstaffnage, Dunollie, besides Oban and fortresses on various islands.

Interestingly, MacDougall of Lorn was

appointed Admiral of the Western Seaboard by Edward II. But it was not until King Robert I's death that any of the forfeited estates were returned. In 1354, however, John MacDougall of Lorn married Robert I's granddaughter, and the family recovered some of its former power.

The MacDougalls supported the Stuarts and in 1715, the MacDougall chief's wife held Dunollie Castle against the Government troops while he was fighting at Sheriffmuir with the Jacobite forces. The estate was confiscated, but restored in the next generation.

The MacDougall Lords of Lorn held Dunstaffnage, the fortified seat of the Kings of Dalriada, in the thirteenth century, but it later passed to the Campbells. They founded the Valliscaulian priory

BELOW *Dunollie Castle, Oban*

MacDougall

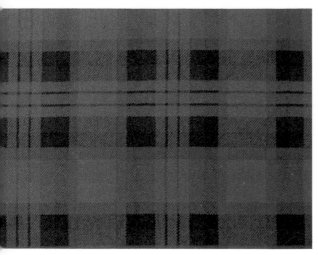

MacDuff Dress Ancient

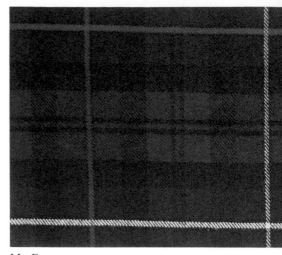

MacEwen

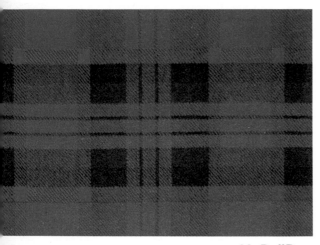

MacDuff Dress

MacDuff Hunting

of Ardchattan in 1231, and held Gylen Castle, Kerrera, in the thirteenth century. Dunollie Castle, Oban, is still maintained by the family.

MacDowall

THE MACDOWELLS of Galloway claim to be descended from the ancient Lords of Galloway. Sir Dugald McDowall was Sheriff of Dumfries and Constable of Dumfries Castle in 1312.

MacDuff

MACDUFF, 1ST EARL OF FIFE, was held to be the Earl of Fife connected with Macbeth. The MacDuffs held the ancient privilege of crowning the kings of Scotland. The old earldom became extinct in 1353 on the death of Duncan, 12th Earl. In 1759 William Duff, Lord Braco, was created Earl of Fife in the Irish peerage. These Earls of Fife built Duff House, Banff (William Adam), and founded the town of Dufftown in 1817, having a barony from Macduff on the Moray Firth. In 1827 James, 4th Earl, was raised to the peerage of Great Britain, and Alexander, 6th of the line, was created Duke of Fife in 1889 when he married Queen Victoria's granddaughter, Princess Louise.

In north-east Fife, at Newburgh, there is the Cross of MacDuff. According to ancient tradition, sanctuary could be claimed here by any kinsman of the MacDuffs.

MacDuffie *see* MacFie, etc.

MacEwen

EWEN OF OTTER lived in the thirteenth century. Swene, last of Otter, granted the lands of Otter to Duncan Campbell in 1432 and resigned the barony of Otter in Argyllshire to James I, from whom it passed to the Campbells.

A large number of MacEwans settled in the Lennox, Lochaber and Galloway. Elspeth MacEwan was the last witch to be put to death in Scotland and was executed in Kirkcudbright in 1698.

MacFarlane

PARLAN OR BAR-THOLOMEW, who lived in the reign of King David Bruce, held territories at the head of Loch Lomond and is believed to be ancestor of this clan. They took their battle cry from Loch Sloy, a small loch under Ben Vorlich which is now part of a hydroelectric scheme.

The MacFarlanes also claim descent from the ancient Celtic earldom of Lennox, from whom they received their lands at Arrochar. They continued to be followers of the Earls of Lennox, but later opposed Mary, Queen of Scots' supporters at Langside in 1568. In the sixteenth century, the MacFarlanes embarked upon a feud with the Colquhouns and in 1592 were responsible for the murder of Sir Humphrey Colquhoun. A further feud developed with the Buchanans and the Clan MacFarlane was generally considered to be a troublesome lot. Through an Act of Estates in 1642 they were deprived of their lands and scattered. By the eighteenth century, however, the Chief was able to build a splendid house at New Tarbert, but the estate was eventually sold in 1784.

MacFarlanes were found latterly at Strathdon in Aberdeenshire, with others at Braemar and Strathspey.

MacFarlane Black and White

MacFarlane

MacFarlane Hunting

The Isle of Colonsay

MacFie, MacPhee, or MacDuffie

A BRANCH OF Clan Alpin, MacDuffie of Colonsay was reported to be hereditary Keeper of the Records of the Lords of the Isles. The MacFies held Colonsay until the mid-seventeenth century and later were scattered through the Clearances. Some followed Lochiel; others the Islay MacDonalds.

On Oronsay there are a number of MacDuffie tombs, but members of the clan are now found all around the world.

MacFie, MacPhee, or MacDuffie

MacFie, MacPhee, or MacDuffie Ancient

145

MacGillivray

ORIGINALLY FROM Morvern and Lochaber, they sought the protection of Mackintosh in the thirteenth century and are therefore identified with Clan Chattan. The MacGillivrays settled in Strathnairn in Inverness-shire and their earliest possession appears to have been Dunmaglass, but they did not have a heritable right to Dunmaglass from the Campbells of Cawdor until 1626.

Alexander, Chief of the clan, led the Clan Chattan Regiment at Culloden and was killed. His brother acquired the estate, and by 1858 it was substantial and passed to the Dalcrombie line who had moved to Canada.

MacGowan *see* Gow

MacGregor

SENIOR CLAN of the Clan Alpin, and said to be descendants of Griogar, third son of Kenneth MacAlpine, King of Scots in the ninth century. At one time they held lands in Perthshire and Argyllshire: Glenstrae, Glenlochy, Glenlyon and Glengyle. They were relieved of these by the powerful Clan Campbell and consequently resorted to violence, becoming raiders and killers.

In 1603, Clan Gregor won a victory over the Colquhouns at Glenfruin. The Colquhouns held a Royal Commission and the victory was considered an act of rebellion. The clan was consequently outlawed. Those who were not hunted down and exterminated were forced to change their name. The persecution continued into the reign of Charles I. When the Marquis of Montrose raised Charles I's standard in 1644, the Laird of MacGregor came forward and joined him. At the Restoration, the MacGregors were pardoned. However, it was not until 1775 that the clan was restored finally to their rightful name. In those 170 years many of the clan had found sanctuary with other clans and had changed their names. It is impossible, therefore, to indicate accurately all the sept names linked with this ancient clan. One of the most notorious of the name was Rob Roy MacGregor (1671–1734) who had Balquhidder Farm. His grave is in the local church. The ancestral burial ground, however, is at Inchcailloch, off Balmaha in Dunbartonshire.

MacGillivray

MacGregor

OPPOSITE *Memorial to the Chief of the MacGillivrays, Culloden Moor*

Loch Katrine in the heart of the Trossachs. The MacGregors hid their stolen cattle here on Ellen's Isle

MacIain

THE MEANING IS 'son of John' – the commonest forename in the Highlands. The MacIains of Ardnamurchan claim descent from a son of Angus Mhor, Lord of the Isles in the fourteenth century. The MacIain MacDonalds were massacred by Government troops in 1692 for failing to sign an allegiance to William of Orange before a given date.

The name appears to have been changed to Johnstone or Johnson, although the reasons for this are obscure.

MacInnes

ORIGINATING FROM the Dalriads, a family of MacInneses were hereditary bowmen to the Chief of Mackinnon. The name means 'son of Angus' and in the seventeenth century a chief of the MacInneses was Keeper of Kinlochaline Castle in Morvern.

MacIntyre

THE 'CHILDREN OF THE CARPENTER' who came from the Hebrides and settled in Lorn in the fourteenth century. They are recorded as having been Hereditary Foresters to the Stewarts of Lorn. The MacIntyres in Badenoch took protection from the Clan Chattan Federation.

It is recorded that they had their estate at Glencoe from 1380 until 1810, but the source of this information is obscure. Before moving to Badenoch, the MacIntyres were listed as followers of the Stewarts of Appin.

Mackay

DESCENT IS CLAIMED from the Royal House of Moray through the line of Morgund of Pluscarden. The clansmen were removed to Ross in 1160 by Malcolm IV and dispersed to Sutherland, where they at one time owned lands from 'Drimholisten to Kylescue'. Other Mackays lived in Galloway and Kintyre.

In 1427, the clan could muster 4000 men, which gives some idea of the strong position they acquired in the land. Their fortunes fluctuated, however, and a period of vassalage to the Huntly Gordons and to the Sutherlands preceded 1628, when Sir Donald Mackay of Strathnaver was made 1st Lord Reay.

Eddrachillis in Sutherland was held by Mackays

MacIntyre Red Ancient

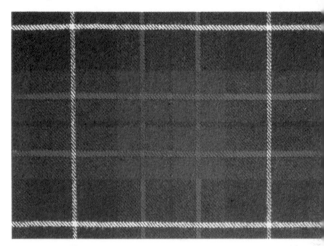

MacIntyre Hunting

MacInnes Hunting

149

from 1515 to 1757. They owned Scourie, and Mackays inhabited Strathnaver until the lands were sold to the Sutherlands in the seventeenth century. Depopulation took place during the notorious Clearances. Tongue House, Kyle of Tongue, was the seat of Lord Reay during the seventeenth and eighteenth centuries, but was sold to the Duke of Sutherland. A Mackays' Society was formed in Glasgow in the early nineteenth century.

Aeneas, 10th Baron Reay, was Minister of State of the Netherlands and created Baron Mackay d'Ophermert of the Netherlands. He died in 1876. Donald, 11th Baron Reay, was Governor of Bombay, 1885–90.

James Lyle Mackay from Arbroath became President of the Bengal Chamber of Commerce, Chairman of the British India Steam Navigation Company and Chairman of P. & O. Steam Navigation Company. He was created 1st Baron Inchcape of Strathnaver and 1st Earl of Inchcape in 1929. Kenneth, 2nd Earl, married Leonora, daughter of HH the Rajah of Sarawak.

Mackellar

THE NAME means son of Ealair, the Gaelic form of the Latin Hilarius, the name of the bishop of Poitiers. The family were well entrenched in Argyllshire from the thirteenth century onwards, but many members moved away overseas or down the west coast to Glasgow.

Archibald McKellar (1884–1901), born in Paisley, won national fame as a sculptor in the United States of America. Kenneth McKellar, the

Paisley-born tenor, is known for his rendition of Scottish songs around the world.

There are families of Mackellar settled in and around Christchurch in New Zealand.

Mackenzie

CLAN MACKENZIE territory was probably much of mid-Ross and around Muir of Orde, but in the twelfth century they were removed to Wester Ross (Kintail) by William the Lion. They were joined by the MacRaes, who became their chief's bodyguard, and the MacLennans, who became their hereditary standard bearers.

In 1263, the battle of Largs terminated the power of the Norsemen in the west, and the Mackenzies were given the right to be part of the Royal Bodyguard, an honour they kept up until the battle of Flodden. Colin Mackenzie, for his services to kings Alexander II and III, was given Royal Charter for the lands of Kintail.

Alexander 'Ionraech', 7th Chief of Kintail, is recorded in the fifteenth century. His grandson, John, fought at Flodden, and John's grandson, Colin, fought for Mary, Queen of Scots at Langside. Colin's eldest son, Kenneth, became Lord Mackenzie of Kintail in 1609, and his descendants include the MacKenzies of Pluscarden and Lochslinn. His eldest son was made 1st Earl of Seaforth in 1623. When he died without issue, the title passed to his half-brother who went to Holland after the execution of Charles I and was later appointed Secretary of State for Scotland. Another of Colin's sons, Sir Ruaridh MacKenzie of Castle Leod, Coigach and Tarbat, was ancestor of the Earls of Cromartie.

After the uprising of 1745, the Earl of Cromartie was condemned to death but was reprieved. For a generation, the Cromartie estates were confiscated and the Earl's son, who had fled overseas, eventually became a Lieutenant-General in Sweden. King George III allowed him to return to Scotland in 1777 and he raised the 71st Highlanders whom he took to India. This regiment became the Highland Light Infantry and was raised before the Seaforth Highlanders (1778). The main Seaforth line died out in 1815 in accordance with a prophecy, made two generations before the Seaforth earldom was created, by 'Coineach Odhar', otherwise known as Kenneth of Kintail or the Brahan Seer. He was burned in oil on Chanonry Point on the Black Isle for dabbling in witchcraft; a memorial to him has recently been erected there.

Tenants of the Seaforth estates were evicted by the Trustees, but were taken in by the Cromartie Mackenzies, who were recognized by the Lord Lyon King of Arms as Chiefs of the Clan Mackenzie.

There have been many distinguished members. Sir Alexander Mackenzie (1764–1820), a Canadian explorer, wrote stirring accounts of his travels across North America; Alexander Mackenzie (1822–92) was a Canadian statesman, born in Perthshire; Sir John Mackenzie (1838–1901), born at Ard-Ross, was an eminent New Zealand statesman; Henry Mackenzie (1745–1831) and Sir Compton Mackenzie (1883–1972) were famous literary members of the clan.

Mackie

A STIRLINGSHIRE NAME that can be traced back to the fifteenth century. The Mackies of mid-Galloway were a powerful and prosperous family of sixteenth- and seventeenth-century Scotland and were enthusiastic supporters of the Covenanters.

Mackinlay.

THE CLAN COUNTRY of the Mackinlays was the Lennox district, but records are obscure. The Mackinlays of Lennox descended from Findlay, a son of Buchanan of Drumikill. Like other Lennox clans, many Mackinlays were also connected with Clan Farquharson, descendants of Farquharson of Braemar in the sixteenth century. There were Findlays or Mackinlays also in Lochalsh and Kintail. Variant spellings of Mackinlay are Donleavy, Finlay, Findlay, Finlayson, Macinally and Mackinley.

The name is also found in the North of Ireland among settlers of the Scots plantation of Ulster. William McKinley (1843–1901), 25th President of the United States of America, was an Ulster Scot.

Mackenzie   Mackinlay

Mackinnon Dress

Mackinnon Hunting

Mackinnon

A BRANCH OF Clan Alpin from Fingon, great-grandson of King Kenneth Mac-Alpine. The Mackinnons were vassals of the Lords of the Isles and were, at times, 'Masters of the Household' and 'Marshals of the Army' for them. For many generations a branch of this family held the post of hereditary Standard Bearer to the MacDonalds of Sleat. Lands on Mull and Strathordell in the Isle of Skye were held, and Dunakin (Castle Maoil), Isle of Skye, was a Mackinnon stronghold from the twelfth to the fifteenth century.

W. Skene states that the Mackinnons were closely connected with the abbacy of Iona. They repeatedly furnished abbots of the monastery although, as was pointed out later, not always to the advantage of the church.

Mackintosh

THE NAME Mackintosh means the 'son of the Thane'. Traditionally, the founder is said to have been a son of MacDuff, ancestor of the Earls of Fife. The Mackintoshes were later connected with the Chiefship of Clan Chattan when Angus, 6th Chief, married Eva, heiress of Clan Chattan, in 1291. Lands in Glenloy and Locharkaig in Lochaber followed, sparking off great feuds with the Earls of Moray and Huntly, and with the Camerons and Gordons. The later additions of Glenroy and Glenspean led to trouble with the MacDonalds of Keppoch.

The clan's feuds were not settled until the late seventeenth century, when Mackintosh gained control of Glenroy and Glenspean, and Cameron of Locheil the superiority of Glenloy and Locharkaig.

The Mackintosh line dwindled and the senior lines died out. The current Chief has his seat at Moy, near Inverness. At Petty parish church on the edge of the Moray Firth is the ancient burial place of the Mackintosh chiefs.

In America, a member of Clan Mackintosh

Castle Maoil, Isle of Skye

Mackintosh   Mackintosh Hunting

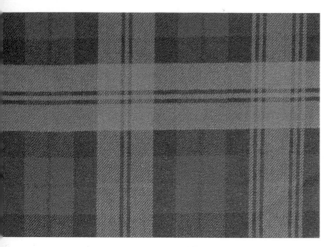

MacLachlan, MacLaughlan

MacLachlan, MacLaughlan Old Sett

MacLachlan, MacLaughlan Dress

married the princess and heiress of the Creek Indian nation.

MacLachlan, MacLaughlan

THE ORIGINAL seat of the Clan MacLachlan would appear to be Lochaber and through marriage they acquired lands in Cowal. Gillespie MacLachlan attended the first parliament of Robert Bruce in 1309. The clan territory is now reduced to a strip on the eastern side of Loch Fyne where the ruins of Castle Lachlan, a twelfth- to thirteenth-century stronghold, can be seen. A cadet branch of the MacLachlans were captains of Innischonnel Castle on Loch Awe from 1613.

MacLaine of Lochbuie

DESCENDED FROM Eachin Reganach, brother of Lachlan Lubanach, who was the ancestor of the Macleans of Duart. The chiefship was settled by tanistry and Duart is recognized as Chief of Clan Maclean, although Eachin Reganach was in fact an elder brother of Lachlan. Charles, son of Eachin, was progenitor of the Macleans of Glen Urquhart and Dochgarroch, a sept of Clan Chattan. The MacLaines were followers of the Lords of the Isles, and were granted lands on Mull. At Loch Buie is Castle Moy, now the ruined keep of what was the seat of the MacLaines of Lochbuie for over 500 years.

See also Maclean.

Maclaren (known also as Clan Labhran)

THERE ARE TWO races of Maclaren, one in Perthshire and the other the Maclaurins, said at one time to have owned the Isle of Tiree. The native clan lands of the former are in Strathearn and Balquhidder. The Maclaren chiefs were hereditary Celtic Abbots of Achtow in Balquhidder. The clan was active in the Jacobite cause in the Risings of 1715 and 1745, and they fought at Culloden. By the late

Waldo E. McIntosh, President Emeritus of Clan Mackintosh (USA), Hereditary Chief of the Creek nation, great grandson of Chief William McIntosh Jr, eldest son of William McIntosh, who came to America from Scotland and married the Princess of the Creek nation

MacLaine of Lochbuie   MacLaine of Lochbuie Hunting

Maclaren (known also as Clan Labhran)

Maclean

THIS CLAN DESCENDS from Gilleain-na-Tuaighe, otherwise Gillean of the Battle Axe, a relative of the Kings of Dalriada, who lived in Moray in the eleventh century. The clan moved westwards and became, at first, staunch supporters of the Lord of Lorn. A dispute, however, allied them to the Lord of the Isles and in 1294 'Gillemoir Mackilyn' was one of the chiefs who signed the Ragman Roll. The clan, therefore, supported Bruce and fought at Bannockburn.

In 1376, a marriage between Chief Lachlan Lubanach to Mary MacDonald, daughter of the Lord of the Isles, brought extensive Mull territories as dowry. Lachlan's elder brother, Eachin Reganach, was to become progenitor of the MacLaines of Lochbuie, but through tanistry Lachlan's line was recognized as the chiefly house. By the fifteenth century, when the Lord of the

eighteenth century the clan was largely dispersed – many of them to Canada.

Achleskine, near the foot of Loch Voil, remained in the chief's family until 1892.

Duart Castle

Maclean Hunting   Maclean of Duart

Isles was forfeited, the Macleans held lands on Tiree, Islay and Jura, in Morvern, Lochaber and Knapdale. These lands were divided among the four main branches: Duart, Ardgour, Coll and Lochbuie. The Macleans prospered and allied with the Campbells of Argyll, strengthening ties through marriage. Lachlan Maclean, however, finding his wife Catherine Campbell incapable of providing him with an heir, chained her to a rock to be drowned by the incoming tide and prematurely reported her death to the Earl of Argyll. Some fishermen rescued her, and in 1523 Lachlan was dirked in his bed while on a visit to Edinburgh.

Feuds continued and in 1598 the powerful Sir Lachlan Mor Maclean was killed in a battle against the MacDonalds on Islay. The clan remained loyal to the Crown throughout the Cromwellian war and Sir Hector Ruadh Maclean died with 500 of his clansmen at Inverkeithing in 1651. The family fell rapidly into debt and were forced to mortgage most of their lands, which were rapidly bought up by the Campbells. In 1674 the Campbells acquired Letters of Fire and Sword and set out to enforce their claims. The Macleans were saved by the Campbells' fall from grace in 1681, but after the Whig Revolution of 1688, Duart was bombarded by English warships, while Sir John Maclean of Duart was fighting for the Jacobites at Killiecrankie.

The Jacobites' defeat enabled the Campbells to seize Duart, and the Macleans were finally suppressed at the battle of Cairnburg Mor in 1691.

Lands forfeited, the direct line of Duart became extinct in 1750 with the death of Sir Hector, 5th

Baronet, and the honours and chiefship devolved upon Alan Maclean of Brolas, next cadet in succession. Colonel Sir Fitzroy Maclean, 10th Baronet and 26th Chief, realized a lifelong ambition and re-acquired Duart Castle in 1911. He died aged 100 having restored the family seat to its former glory.

Sir Fitzroy Maclean

157

Loch Assynt and Ardvreck Castle

Sir Fitzroy was succeeded by his grandson, Sir Charles Maclean, who became Chief Scout of the Commonwealth and Lord Lieutenant of Argyll. In 1971 he was created a Life Peer when he was appointed Lord Chamberlain of Her Majesty's Household.

An infamous clansman was James Maclean, the 'gentleman highwayman'. Born in 1724, he squandered his fortune and took to highway rob-bery. He robbed the Salisbury Flying Coach, Lord Eglinton on Hounslow Heath, and held up Horace Walpole in Hyde Park. He was arrested and after a notable trial hanged at Tyburn in 1730. A visitor to Duart remarked that this must be 'Old Jamie', a skeleton still used by one of London's teaching hospitals.

John Maclean, son of the Laird of Duart, made a large fortune in Sweden in the seventeenth

World. Many emigrated to Canada and the Carolinas. John MacLaine, born in Lennoxtown in 1852, was to become Governor of New Hampshire. Andrew McLean, born in Dunbartonshire in 1848, was founder and editor of the *Brooklyn Citizen*. There is an active Clan Maclean Society in the United States.

See also MacLaine.

Maclellan

'SON OF the servant of St Fillan'. Maclellans were numerous in Galloway towards the end of the fourteenth century, and they gave their name to Balmaclellan in the Stewartry. Lands were granted to John Maclellan by James III. In the reign of David II, Gilbert McGillolane appears as Captain of Glenconnan in Galloway.

Some Maclellans in the Aberfeldy district of Perthshire are regarded as a sept of Clan MacNab.

MacLennan *see* Logan

MacLeod

THIS CLAN descends from Leod, son of Olaf the Black, King of the Isle of Man. He was fostered by Paul Balkasson, Sheriff of Skye, and about 1220 married the daughter and heiress of MacRaild.

Leod had four sons: the eldest, Tormod (Norman), inherited Dunvegan and the Isle of Harris, becoming chief of these lands and adopting the title MacLeod of Dunvegan. The second son, Torquil, inherited Lewis. This branch eventually failed in the male line and is now represented by the MacLeods of Raasay.

The MacLeods served under the Lords of the Isles, holding high rank. Throughout their history, the MacLeods have had many outstanding chiefs. In more recent years Dame Flora MacLeod of MacLeod, who died in 1977 aged 98, did much to publicize the clan by visiting clansfolk all over the world, helping to found clan societies in Canada,

century. He was involved there in the building of the city of Gothenburg and was ennobled by Queen Christina in 1649.

The distinguished diplomat and author, Sir Fitzroy Maclean, belongs to another branch of the family.

When the clan scattered at the end of the seventeenth century, many clansmen found their way down the west coast and overseas to the New

Dame Flora MacLeod

MacLeod Dress   MacLeod Hunting

Australia, New Zealand and the United States.

The MacLeods of Assynt in Sutherland are considered by many to have been the 'black sheep' of the family, for it was to Assynt that the noble Marquess of Montrose fled; and in 1650 after the battle at Carbisdale it was MacLeod of Assynt who betrayed him.

Macmillan

A TRIBE OF MORAY who derived from the ancient people of Kanteai, one of the subsidiaries of the northern Picts. They held lands on Tayside, and Malcolm Mor Macmillan was established in Knapdale with a charter from the Lord of the Isles by 1360. Most of these lands, however, appear to have

Macmillan Ancient Colours

Finlayston House

Macmillan

Macmillan Hunting

MacNab

Harold Macmillan, 1st Earl of Stockton

been lost by the close of the fifteenth century. The Macmillans spread from Knapdale south into Kintyre, and to Galloway and Kirkcudbrightshire.

The seat of the Chief is now at Finlayston House on the Firth of Clyde.

Kirkpatrick Macmillan, the inventor of the bicycle, was born at Keir, at Sanquhar in Nithsdale. He rode his invention to Glasgow and was fined for knocking over a pedestrian. Harold Macmillan, British Prime Minister who became 1st Earl of Stockton, was descended from Malcolm MacMillan, a crofter on Arran in the eighteenth century.

MacNab

THIS CLAN originates from the Hereditary Celtic Abbot of Glendochart in the reign of David I. Early lands were on the shores of Loch Tay, in Strath-fillan and Glen Dochart. The family emigrated to Canada in 1823 and settled in MacNab, near Ottawa. Some of them later returned and the Chief set-

tled at Killin. The MacNabs had burial grounds by the Falls of Dochart in Perthshire.

MacNaughton

MacNaughton Ancient Colours

MacNaughton

IN THE THIRTEENTH CENTURY this clan was found in Lochawe, Glenaray, Glenshire and Loch Fyne. Gillechrist MacNachdan was granted the keeping of the castle of Frechelen (Fraoch Eilean) by Alexander III in 1267. In the fourteenth century, Dundarave became the clan stronghold.

The last MacNaughton of Dundarave was married under alcoholic influence to the wrong daughter of Sir James Campbell of Ardkinglas in 1700. On discovering the mistake the following morning, he fled with the second daughter leaving his wife pregnant. Consequently, Campbell of Ardkinglas acquired MacNaughton's lands.

MacNeil of Colonsay

MacNeil

THE MACNEILS claim descent directly from Niall of the Nine Hostages, High King of Ireland, who came to Barra in 1049. Gilleonan Roderick Murchaid Mac-Neil received a charter for the island from Alexander, Lord of the Isles, in 1427. A branch of the clan acquired Colonsay and Oronsay from the Campbells.

MacNeil of Barra

163

MacNeil of Barra Ancient

Barra was sold in 1838. The estate, however, was bought back and Kisimul Castle, the clan stronghold, restored by Robert Lister Macneil, whose family had moved to America.

In Knapdale are the ruins of Castle Sween where the MacNeils of Gigha were hereditary keepers.

Kisimul Castle

MacNicol *see* Nicholson

MacPhee *see* MacFie, etc.

Macpherson

THE CLAN Macpherson derives its name from Duncan, Parson of Kingussie in the fifteenth century, himself a descendant of Muriach, Chief of Clan Chattan in 1173. Three brothers, Kenneth, John and Gillies, who lived in the mid-fourteenth century, are believed to be the ancestors of the Macphersons of Cluny, Pitmain and Invershie, respectively. In the Rising of 1745, Cluny Macpherson transferred his loyalties to the Jacobites, and for nine years following the disaster at Culloden Moor dodged the Government troops who sought him.

The Cluny estate, restored in 1784, eventually comprised most of Laggan and although lost dur-

BAGH A CHAISTEIL

Macpherson Dress   Macpherson

ing the Second World War, several acres have
been settled in perpetuity as a clan rallying ground.

Near Kingussie is the house of Balavil, built by
James Macpherson, so-called translator of the
fabled Ossian poems. At Newtonmore there is a
Clan Macpherson museum.

MacQuarrie

A BRANCH OF Clan Alpin
who had a territory on the
islands of Mull and Ulva.
Followers of the Lords of
the Isles, most of the family
papers were burned in a
fire in 1688. Ulva was sold
for financial reasons in
1777. It is known that the
island of Staffa was once
part of the MacQuarrie
estate and Gruline House,
Salen, on the Isle of Mull, was the home of Major-
General Lachlan Macquarrie (1761–1824), first
Governor of New South Wales.

MacQuarrie

Macqueen

DESCENDED FROM 'Conn of the Hundred Battles', as are the MacDonalds, the Macqueens of
Garafad held lands on the island of Skye for many
centuries. The clan always maintained a close
relationship with Clan Donald, although they
eventually became associated with Clan Chattan
through the marriage of Mora MacDonald of
Moidart to the 10th Chief of Mackintosh. From
then on the Macqueens were known as Clan
Revan, from a kinsman of the bride, a certain

Macqueen

165

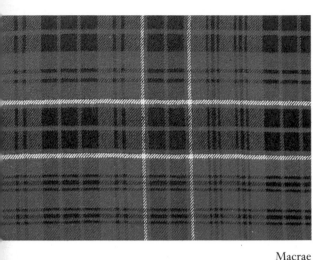

Macrae

Macrae of Conchra

Revan MacMulmor MacAngus Macqueen.

From the fifteenth until the eighteenth century, Corrybrough estate, near Tomatin, belonged to Clan Revan.

Macrae

THE NAME means 'Son of Grace' in Gaelic. The Macraes are said to have settled in Kintail in the fourteenth century, and they became Chamberlains of Kintail for several generations under the Mackenzies.

Eilean Donan on the Kyle of Lochalsh was built in the thirteenth century and held by the Macraes as Constables for the Earls of Seaforth. The castle serves as a war memorial for the Clan Macrae.

MacThomas

THOMAS, A GAELIC-SPEAKING Highlander, known as Tomaidh Mor ('Great Tommy'), was a descendant of the Clan Chattan Mackintoshes. He lived in the fifteenth century at a time when the Clan Chattan Federation had become large and unmanageable, so he took his kinsmen and followers across the Grampians from Badenoch to Glenshee. Iain Mor, 7th Chief, joined Montrose at Dundee in 1644. The clan scattered after his death.

Early chiefs had settled at the Thom, on the east side of the Shee Water, opposite the Spittal of Glenshee. The MacThomas Gathering Ground is located here. In about 1600, the 4th Chief, Robert McComie of the Thom, was murdered. The chiefship passed to his brother, John McComie of Finegand, which is situated about 3 miles down Glenshee.

Maitland

A LOWLAND FAMILY who rose to become Dukes of Lauderdale and played important roles in Scottish affairs for generations.

Sir John Maitland adhered to the Queen's party in 1567 and his office was forfeit. He was reappointed a Lord of Session in 1581 and became Secretary of State for life in 1584 with the title of Vice-Chancellor. He was created 1st Lord of Thirlestane. His son, the 2nd Lord, became President of the Council and was created Earl of Lauderdale in 1624. John, 2nd Earl, was a

MacThomas

Eilean Donan Castle

staunch supporter of Charles II and was made Secretary of State, Lord High Commissioner to the Parliament and Governor of Edinburgh Castle. In 1672, he was created 1st Duke of Lauderdale, and in 1674, 1st Earl of Guildford. At his death all the titles conferred upon him became extinct, and the earldom reverted to his brother, Charles, who became General of the Mint.

John Maitland of Thirlestane built Thirlestane Castle, Lauder, and it was enlarged by the 1st Duke of Lauderdale. From the fourteenth century, the Maitlands lived at Lethington, which was bought in the eighteenth century by Lord Blantyre who renamed the castle Lennoxlove. Queensberry House in Edinburgh's Canongate, which is now a hospital, was built for Charles Maitland, 3rd Earl, in 1681.

The earls of Lauderdale are Hereditary Saltire Banner Bearers of Scotland.

Malcolm

THE NAME means a devotee of St Columba, and four Scottish kings carried this name. Malcolumb is recorded in a charter of 1094.

Maiklum was an old surname in Strathblane, but it is found throughout Scotland.

John Malcolm of Balbedie, Lochore and Innertiel was appointed Chamberlain of Fife in 1641. His eldest son was created a Nova Scotia baronet in 1665, and his third son became Senator of the College of Justice with the name of Lord Lochore.

See also MacCallum.

John
Duke of Lauderdale

OPPOSITE
Thirlestane Castle

RIGHT *1st Duke
of Lauderdale by
Sir Peter Lely*

Maitland   Malcolm

Northfield House, Prestonpans

Marjoriebanks

WALTER, HIGH STEWARD of Scotland, married Marjorie, only daughter of Robert Bruce, and the barony of Ratho in Renfrewshire was granted by the king to his daughter. These lands were denominated 'Terrae de Rath Marjorie banks', hence the name which was acquired by a family called Johnstone, who held lands in Dumfriesshire. Balbardie House, in Bathgate, was a Marjoriebanks residence, undermined by subterranean tunnelling for coal and demolished in 1957 – all save the west wing which remains amid modern houses. Joseph Marjoriebanks, an Edinburgh merchant, built the splendid Northfield House at Prestonpans in 1611.

Matheson, Mathieson

THE NAME means 'Son of the Bear'. The clan is an early offshoot of the Celtic Earls of Ross and is said to have come from Lochalsh. There were two main branches: Lochalsh and Shinness, Sutherland. From the former descend the Mathesons of Attadale and Ardross.

The Mathesons were involved in the sixteenth century with other clans who settled in Lochalsh, and in particular the

170

Matheson, Mathieson   Matheson, Mathieson Hunting

MacDonnells of Glengarry and the Mackenzies of Kintail.

Alexander Matheson of Lochalsh was created a baronet in 1882. The 3rd Baronet had three sons, all of whom were killed during the First World War.

Maule

THIS FAMILY descended from the de Maules who possessed the *seigneurie* of that name in the department of Seine-et-Oise in France. The first of that name in Scotland appears to be Robert, who probably came north with David I. He received grants of lands in the Lothians, possibly Mauldslie in Temple. Robert's son William took part in the battle of the Standard in 1138 and obtained the lands of Easter Fowlis in Perthshire. By marriage between Peter de Maule and Christina de Valoniis before 1215, the family acquired the baronies of Panmure and Bervie.

Panmure House, built after 1661 and demolished in 1955, stood at Carnoustie. The gates, which survive, have not been opened since the 4th Earl of Panmure fled to France in 1715, after supporting the Old Pretender. The pillar on the hill to the west of Carnoustie commemorates Lord Panmure of Brechin who died in 1852. The 2nd son of the 8th Earl of Dalhousie changed his name to Maule in 1831 after he had been created

Lord Panmure. The 2nd Baron Panmure inherited the earldom of Dalhousie from his cousin in 1860 and assumed the name of Ramsay. The barony of Panmure disappeared when his cousin inherited the Dalhousie earldom in 1874.

The Earls of Dalhousie live at Brechin Castle. In 1303, during the invasion of Edward I of England, the castle was strong enough to withstand siege for three weeks, surrendering only after its governor, Sir Thomas Maule, had been killed.

Maxtone

FROM THE BARONY of Maxton in Roxburghshire. It is suggested that the name came from Maccus, the son of Undewyn, who in the reign of David I obtained lands in that area. The barony passed to the Berkeleys and later to the de Normanvilles. The Hungarian family of similar name is related to an individual of this name who emigrated from Scotland. A family of Maxtons settled in Cultoquhey in Perthshire and one of its members was responsible for the famous litany commenting on the characteristics of various Scottish clans written in 1725.

James Maxton (1885–1946), the outspoken Clydeside Labour Member of Parliament of earlier this century, is a famous representative of this name. He was born in Barrhead, Glasgow.

171

Maxwell

SIR JOHN MAXWELL, Chamberlain of Scotland in the thirteenth century, seems to be the first recorded of the name. The Maxwells held lands in Annandale and became Lords Maxwell and Earls of Nithsdale; and for many years they were Wardens of the West March, and Stewards of Annandale and Kircudbright. Prominent families are those of Pollok, Cardoness, Monreith and Farnham.

The 1st Baronet of Monreith, Wigtownshire, was created in 1681. The 7th Baronet was a Lord of the Treasury, 1886–92.

The branch of the family descended from the Earls of Nithsdale is the Maxwells of Pollok, on the outskirts of Glasgow. A Sir John Maxwell of Pollok distinguished himself at an early age by capturing Sir Ralph Percy, son of the Earl of Northumberland, at Otterburn.

Caerlaverock Castle, south of Dumfries, was the thirteenth-century stronghold of the Maxwells and, as such, besieged by Edward I of England.

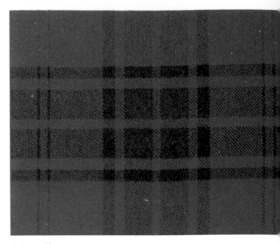

Maxwell

Monreith Tower, west of Whithorn in Wigtownshire, was where the writer Gavin Maxwell, one of the descendants of the Monreith branch, grew up; there is a memorial to him on a hill overlooking Monreith Bay. Pollok House, eighteenth-century home of the Maxwells of Pollok, was gifted by the Stirling-Maxwell family to Glasgow in 1967. The famous Burrell Collection is housed in a purpose-built museum in the grounds.

Caerlaverock Castle

Melville

FROM THE BARONY of Malaville in Normandy: Galfridus de Malveill appears in Scotland in the twelfth century. Sir Robert Melville was twice Ambassador to England, Hereditary Keeper of Linlithgow Palace, Vice-Chancellor, and an Extraordinary Lord of Session with the title of Lord Murdocairnie (1594–1601). He was later created 1st Lord Monymaill. The 2nd Lord, an Extraordinary Lord of Session as Lord Burntisland, 1601–8, obtained a new charter of the lordship with remainders to his heirs general bearing the name of Melville.

George, 4th Lord, who supported the Duke of Monmouth, was attainted but escaped to Holland, returning with William and Mary of Orange in 1688, and the following year he was created 1st Earl of Melville. He was Secretary of State, High Commissioner to Parliament, 1690, and President of the Council, 1696. He married Lady Catherine Leslie, daughter of the 2nd Earl of Leven, and their son, David, 2nd Earl of Melville, had also succeeded as 3rd Earl of Leven in 1682.

Andrew Melville (1542–1622) was a scholar, theologian and reformer. He became Rector of St Andrews University, having been Principal of St Mary's College, St Andrews, and before that Principal of Glasgow University (1574). He spent four years in the Tower of London and passed his remaining years in France as professor at the University of Sedan. It is interesting to note that in his own diary he spells his name both Melville and Melvin, even on the same page.

Menzies

A NORMAN FAMILY who came from Mayneris, near Rouen. The earliest definitive Chief was Sir Robert de Meygners who became Chamberlain of Scotland in 1249. Records of the early history of the Menzies family were lost in a fire which destroyed their first castle at Weem in 1592, but it is probable that a branch

Menzies Dress

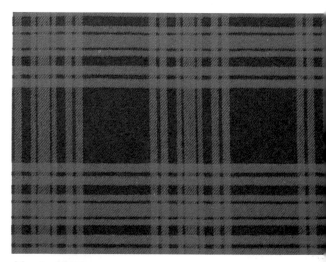

Menzies Hunting

Menzies Black and White

of the family was granted lands in the Lothians in the twelfth century and eventually became established in the central Highlands. Extensive lands from Glendochart to Aberfeldy were granted to Sir Alexander Meygners, son of Sir Robert, for services to Robert Bruce. Bruce later bestowed upon Sir Alexander the baronies of Glendochart and Durisdeer.

In later years, the main Menzies territories were around Weem, the Appin of Dull and Rannoch, and branches of the line became established at Pitfoddels in Aberdeenshire, Durisdeer in Nithsdale, Shian in Glenquaich, Culdares in Glenlyon, Rotmell at Dalmally in Perthshire, Vogrie in Midlothian and Culter at Lanark.

Castle Menzies, north-west of Aberfeldy, was erected in the latter part of the sixteenth century and it is now owned by the Clan Menzies Society, who open it to the public.

Moncreiffe

THE NAME is taken from the lands of Moncreiffe which were gifted by Alexander II in 1248 to Sir Matthew Moncreiffe, who also held lands in Strathearn, Fife and Atholl, and who possibly descended from Duncan I's brother, Maldred (killed 1045). In 1568, William of that Ilk, 11th Chief, entered into a treaty with 'the haill Name of Murray' for their mutual defence.

Sir Thomas Moncreiffe was Clerk of the Exchequer and Treasury during the reigns of Charles II, James VII and II, and William and Mary. He inherited the family estate.

Moncreiffe

Sir Iain Moncreiffe of that Ilk, Albany Herald and distinguished historian who died in 1985

Montgomerie

Montgomerie Green

Sir Iain Moncreiffe of that Ilk also inherited his title and lands from a kinsman, and was Albany Herald at the court of the Lord Lyon. In 1946, he married the only child of the 22nd Earl of Erroll, who consequently had become a Countess in her own right. On her death, the earldom passed to their eldest son along with the Moncreiffe baronetcy. Their second son, the Hon. Peregrine Moncreiffe, will eventually become Chief of the Name in succession to his cousin Miss Elizabeth Moncreiffe.

Montgomerie

ROGER DE MONT-GOMERIE, born about 1030, was joint Regent of Normandy when William the Conqueror invaded England in 1066. He was created Earl of Arundel.

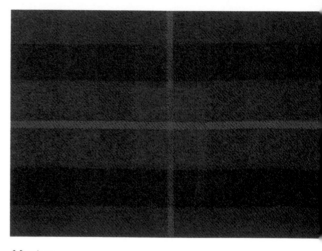

Morrison

The first of the family in Scotland appears to be Robert de Mundegumerie, who died about 1177. He was granted Eaglesham in Renfrewshire and his descendant married the heiress of Sir Hugh de Eglinton.

Sir Alexander Montgomerie was created 1st Lord Montgomerie in 1449. After the fall of James IV at Flodden, the 3rd Lord was nominated one of the Queen-Dowager's Councillors and was created Earl of Eglinton in 1508. The 5th Earl obtained a charter settling the Eglinton earldom on his cousin, Alexander Seton, third son of the 1st Earl of Winton. In 1840, the 13th Earl of Eglinton was served as heir male to the 4th Earl of Winton.

Eglinton Castle, north of Irvine, was built in 1798. Skelmorlie Castle, Largs, was restored in 1852, but the oldest part dates back to 1502.

Morrison

SAID TO BE of Scandinavian origin, possibly from a natural son of a king of Norway who was cast ashore on the Isle of Lewis on a piece of driftwood. The Morrisons held the Hereditary Brieveship (Judges of the Island) of Lewis until 1613. They were deadly enemies of the Lewis MacAulays.

For their various services, they were given the lands around Ness in Lewis. There were Morrisons in the counties of Perth, Stirling and Dunbarton, but they had no family connection with the Lewis Morrisons.

Mowat

Muir

Mowat

SAID TO HAVE SETTLED in Scotland in the reign of King David I, they were of Norman origin and moved to the north-east of Scotland, Orkney and Shetland. Hatton Castle at Turriff, built in the thirteenth century, belonged to the Mowats until 1723. There is said to have been a feud between the Mowats and the Camerons. The Mowats of Abergeldie agreed to settle the dispute at the Woods of Brux, near Alford, in a combat which took place with twelve horsemen on each side. The Mowats arrived with two men on each horse and massacred the Camerons.

The first record of the name in Scotland appears to be Robert de Montealto, who arrived from Wales, where the family had first settled. One of the family accompanied Alexander III's daughter, Princess Margaret, to Norway in the thirteenth century, but it appears that on the return journey the ship was wrecked and the crew and passengers were all drowned.

Mowats were settled in Ayrshire as early as 1400 and from the seventeenth century they are found in Edinburgh.

Muir

THOMAS DE LA MORE was executor of the will of Dervorguilla de Balliol, the heiress daughter of Alan, Earl of Galloway, and mother of King John Balliol, chosen by Edward I of England as King of Scots. The Muirs of More held lands in Ayrshire, Lanarkshire and Beltone in Berwickshire. Elizabeth Mure, daughter of Sir Adam Mure of Rowallan, married Robert II in 1347. The family of Muir of Rowallan became extinct in the male line in 1700.

Alexander Muir, created baronet in 1805, descended from the Muirs of Cassencarrie and assumed the additional name of Mackenzie upon succeeding to the estates of his great-uncle, John Mackenzie of Delvine, Perthshire, third son of the 1st Baronet of Coul. Sir John Muir of Deanston, Perthshire, created baronet in 1892, was Lord Provost of Glasgow, 1889–92. This family owned Blair Drummond, by Stirling.

Munro

A ROSS-SHIRE CLAN, ancient vassals of the Earls of Ross and originally from North Moray. The first Chief was Hugh who lived in the twelfth century. William, 12th of Foulis, was knighted by James IV. The clan lands near Dingwall were called Ferindonald, after the supposed founder of the clan. The Munros supported the Government in the Jacobite risings.

Foulis Castle, north of Dingwall, is the eighteenth-century seat of the Chief. A condition of the clan's tenure was that a snowball should be presented to the reigning monarch when passing. This could be obtained from nearby Ben Wyvis, never completely without snow.

Major-General Sir Thomas Munro, KCB, of Lindertis, Forfarshire, was Governor of Madras, 1820–7. General Sir Hector Munro (1726–1805) of Navar House, near Evanton, built a structure supposedly representing the gateway to an Indian town on the top of Knock Fyrish (1483 ft). He paid local people to carry the stones up the hill as a way of easing local unemployment.

Murray

FRESKIN DE MORAVIA of Duffus, in Moray, acquired lands from David I, his ancestor. He appears to have been chieftain of the Duffus branch of the Royal House of Moray. William de Moravia, his grandson, married the heiress of Bothwell and Drumsagard in Lanarkshire, and Smailholm in Berwickshire. From their son descend the Murrays of Tullibardine, ancestors of the Dukes of Atholl.

Sir John Murray, 12th Feudal baron of Tullibardine, was created 1st Lord Murray of Tullibardine in 1604, then 1st Earl of Tullibardine in 1606. William, 2nd Earl, who rescued James VI at Perth in the Gowrie Conspiracy, married Lady Dorothea Stewart, daughter of John, 5th Stewart

Munro

Munro Ancient

177

Murray of Athol

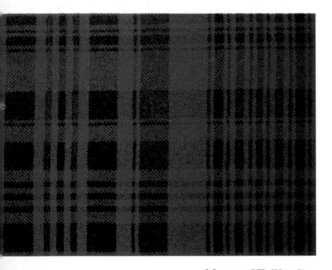

Murray of Tullibardine

Earl of Atholl. The earldoms of Atholl and Tullibardine merged in 1607 and, in 1676, the 2nd Earl of Atholl and 5th Earl of Tullibardine was created 1st Marquess of Atholl. The 2nd Marquess was created 1st Duke of Atholl in 1703, but his eldest son, having supported the Earl of Mar in 1715, was attainted. James, 2nd Duke, upon whom the family honours were settled by Act of Parliament, also succeeded to the barony of Strange through his grandmother, and, in addition, to the sovereignty of the Isle of Man, which was disposed of to the British Government by the 3rd Duke for £70,000. The seat of the Dukes of Atholl is Blair Castle, Blair Atholl. The castle dates back to 1269. Mary, Queen of Scots, and Prince Charles Edwart Stuart stayed here, and it was besieged by Lord George Murray while it was occupied by Hanoverian forces in 1745. The Duke of Atholl maintains the only legal private army in Scotland, the Atholl Highlanders.

Sir David Murray, Captain of the Guard for James VI of Scotland, accompanied that king to England, and was created 1st Viscount Stormont in 1621. William Murray, third son of the 5th Viscount Stormont, Lord Chief Justice of England, was created 1st Earl of Mansfield in 1776. This family's home is at Scone Palace, Perth. The second son of the 1st Marquess of Atholl was Master of the Horse to Queen Mary II of England and was created 1st Earl of Dunmore in 1686.

Other branches of the clan include the Murrays of Blackbarony, Dunerne, Octertyre and Abercairney, and the Lords Elibank.

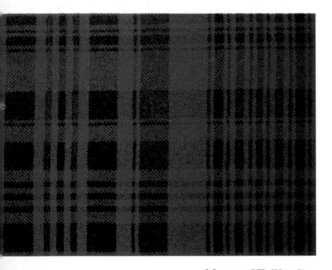

Murray of Tullibardine Ancient

178

OPPOSITE *Blair Castle*

Napier

Napier

A NAME RECORDED in Scotland as early as 1140, but the heraldry of the Napiers of Merchiston shows a descent from the Lennox family. The Napiers of Napier in Renfrewshire claim this descent and the name is said to derive from Alexander III's statement after a battle that 'Lennox had na peer', in other words, no equal.

Lord Napier, son of John Napier (1550–1617) the inventor of logarithms, married the 1st Marquess of Montrose's sister and lived at the

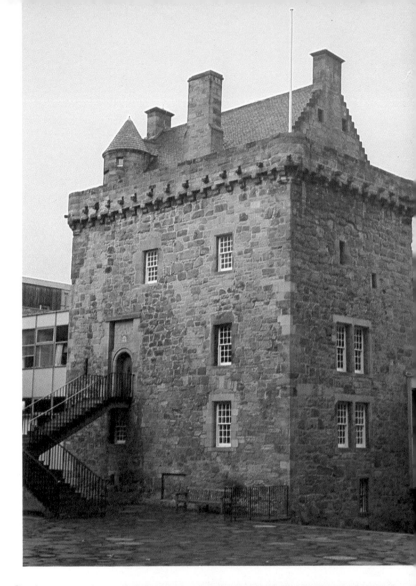

OPPOSITE *Scone Palace*

RIGHT *Merchiston Castle, Edinburgh*

fifteenth-century Merchiston Castle, now restored and used as the nucleus for Napier College, Edinburgh. Sir Archibald Napier of Merchiston built the sixteenth-century tower which is incorporated in the later Lauriston Castle on the north side of Edinburgh.

Nicholson or MacNicol

THE NAME arose in the Lowlands of Scotland around Dumfries and in Glasgow, but it is also found in the islands of Skye and Lewis, as a form of MacNicol. In 1629, John Nicolson of Lasswade was created a baronet of Nova Scotia, and he is said to be a descendant of the Dean of Brechin in Angus. Sir William Nicolson of Lasswade, who died in 1766, married four times, and is said to have fathered twenty-three children.

Nicholson or MacNicol

181

Nisbet

FROM THE OLD BARONY of Nesbit in Berwickshire. The name is first recorded in the twelfth century. Philip Nesbitt of that Ilk was a sheriff in 1493 and Thomas of Nesbitt was a prior of Coldingham from 1446 to 1456. Some Nesbitts went to Sweden in the sixteenth century and there are many of their descendants now living in that country.

James Nisbet was a distinguished architect-plasterer at the end of the eighteenth century. Alexander Nisbet wrote the authoritative work on Scots heraldry, *A System of Heraldry*, in 1722.

Ogilvy

GILLIBRIDE, SECOND SON of Ghillechriost, Earl of Angus, is the ancestor of this clan. He received the barony of Ogilvy in the parish of Glamis in about 1163. Sir Patrick de Ogilvy acquired the lands of Kettins in Angus and his descendant, Sir Walter, was appointed the Hereditary Sheriff of Angus.

Sir James Ogilvy, Scottish Ambassador to Denmark, was created 1st Lord Ogilvy of Airlie and died in 1504. James, 7th Lord, a supporter of Charles I, was created 1st Earl of Airlie in 1639. James, 2nd Earl, taken prisoner at the battle of Philiphaugh in 1644, was sentenced to death at St Andrews, but escaped before his intended execution. Airlie lands included Glenisla, Glenprosen and Glenclova in Angus. Airlie Castle, Kirriemuir, has been an Ogilvy stronghold since 1430, but was superseded by a mansion in 1763. Cortachy Castle has been held by the Ogilvys of Airlie since the seventeenth century.

Sir Walter Ogilvie was created Baron Ogilvie of Deskford in 1616. The 2nd Baron was created 1st Earl of Findlater in 1638. In 1701 James, son of the 3rd Earl of Findlater, was created 1st Earl of Seafield.

Branches include the Ogilvys of Inverquharity in Forfarshire, a Nova Scotia baronetcy, and the Ogilvys of Winton Castle, East Lothian.

OPPOSITE *Lauriston Castle, Edinburgh*

In 1963 the Hon. Angus Ogilvy, second son of the 12th Earl of Airlie, married Princess Alexandra, daughter of Prince George, Duke of Kent, and Princess Marina, Duchess of Kent.

Oliphant

THE FAMILY held lands in Northamptonshire, and were of Norman origin. They were associated with David I, and William Holifard saved David at the rout of Winchester in 1141, for which he received with land in Scotland. David Olifard, godson of David I, acquired lands in Roxburghshire. Sir William

Ogilvy

Ogilvy of Airlie

183

Oliphant was the commander who held Stirling Castle against the siege by Edward I of England. The Oliphants received lands at Gask and Aberdalgie from Robert Bruce and the title of Lord Oliphant was conferred in 1458.

Kellie Castle at Pittenweem in Fife belonged to the Oliphants for 250 years until 1613, when it was acquired by the Erskines. Hatton Castle at Newtyle in Angus was built by Laurence, 14th Lord Oliphant, in 1575. The lands at Ardblair, near Blairgowrie, were granted to Thomas Blair by David II, but passed by marriage to the Oliphants of Gask.

Preston

FROM THE BARONY of Preston, now known as Craigmillar in Edinburgh. Alured de Preston is recorded in Scotland in the thirteenth century. There is no doubt of a historic connection with the de Preston family of Ireland who became Viscounts Gormanston.

Sir John de Preston, taken prisoner at the battle of Durham in 1346, had obtained a charter for lands at Gorton in 1342. One William Preston brought the arm bone of St Giles from France and gifted it to the church of St Giles. Sir Simon Preston of Craigmillar was Provost of Edinburgh in the sixteenth century and this line came to an end with the death of Sir Robert Preston in 1639.

Pringle

FROM THE LANDS of this name in Roxburghshire. The name appears in the reign of Alexander III. A Pringle was Constable of Cessford in the sixteenth century and the Pringles were numbered among the Riding Clans of the Scottish Borders. The Pringles of Stichill, Roxburghshire, acquired a Nova Scotia baronetcy in 1683.

Ramsay

A FAMILY OF ancient Anglo-Norman origin; the first recorded in Scotland was Simon de Ramsay, who was granted lands in Lothian by David I. Sir John Ramsay of Dalhousie and Melrose was created Lord Ramsay of Melrose in 1618. William, 2nd Baron, was created 1st Earl of Dalhousie in 1633 after the battles of Marston Moor and Philiphaugh. The 9th Earl was Governor-General of Canada (1819–28), and the 10th Earl was Governor-General of India (1847–56). The present Earl was Governor-General of the Federation of Rhodesia and Nyasaland, 1967–73, and Lord Chamberlain to HM Queen Elizabeth, the Queen Mother. The

Ramsay

Dalhousie Castle

Ramsays of Banff, Perthshire, who acquired a Novia Scotia baronetcy in 1666, are descended in the male line from Neis de Ramsay, physician to Alexander II. Sir Alexander, 1st Baronet of Balmain, Kincardineshire, was the second son of Sir Thomas Burnett, but succeeded his uncle in the Ramsay estates in 1806 and changed his name.

Dalhousie Castle, Midlothian, was owned by the Ramsays from the thirteenth century, but is now a hotel. Through marriage with the de Maule family, the Earls of Dalhousie acquired Brechin Castle in Angus.

Queen Victoria's granddaughter, Princess Patricia of Connaught and Strathearn, married the Hon. Alexander Ramsay, a son of the 13th Earl of Dalhousie, in 1919. She asked to relinquish her royal title and was known thereafter as Lady Patricia Ramsay of Mar.

Rattray

A FOLLOWER, but not a sept, of the Murrays of Atholl. The family descends from Adam de Rattrieff, who lived in the thirteenth century. Their ancient seat is at Craighall, Blairgowrie, in Perthshire.

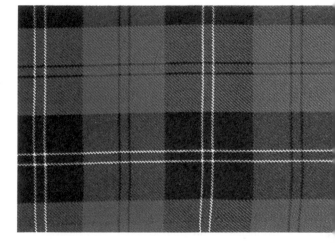

Ramsay Blue

Rattray

185

Robertson or Donnachaidh

DUNCAN OR DON-NACHAIDH REAMHAIR, who led the clan for Robert Bruce at Bannockburn, was descended from the Celtic Earls of Atholl. From a later Chief, Robert, in the reign of James I, comes the name of Robertson. The barony of Struan was granted to Robert Duncanson by James II. The Robertsons rallied to the Stuart banner for the Marquess of Montrose and in the Jacobite risings. The clan seat was at Dunalastair in Kinloch Rannoch and the Rannoch Barracks built by Hanoverian troops, c. 1751, was intended to control Clan Robertson. There is a Clan Donnachaidh museum at Bruar Falls in Blair Atholl.

Branches were Woodsheal, Lude, Faskally, Straloch and Delcaber.

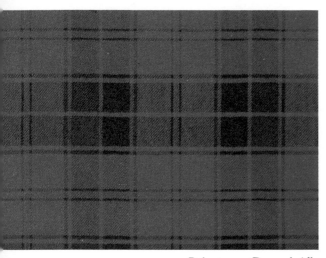

Robertson or Donnachaidh

Robertson or Donnachaidh Hunting

Rollo

TWO FORMS of this name are found in Perthshire and Fife. However, lands of Duncrub were granted to John Rollo in 1380.

Sir Andrew Rollo was created Baron Rollo of Duncrub in 1651. Robert, 4th Baron, supported the Old Pretender in 1715, but surrendered. The 5th Baron served as a

Rollo

Brigadier-General in the American War of Independence.

Rose

THE FAMILY of Rose of Kilravock settled in Nairn in the reign of King David I. Kilravock Castle, Nairn, was built in 1460 by Hugh Rose of Kilravock. It was added to in the seventeenth century and Prince Charles Edward Stuart was entertained here before the battle of Culloden in 1745 – while the Duke of Cumberland slept in a town house in Nairn. Interestingly, the Roses were not Jacobites and consistently supported the Government in 1688, 1715 and 1745, although the 15th Chief had opposed the Act of Union in 1707.

Colonel Sir Hugh Rose of Leith was created a baronet in 1935, having been Chairman of Clyde, Paper & Co Ltd, paint manufacturers, and Honorary Colonel of the Forth Heavy Brigade, RA (Territorial Army).

Ross

SAID TO BE of Norman origin, but probably descended from Gilleon na h-airde, ancestor of Anrias, whose descendant Fearcher MacinTagart, Earl of Ross, helped crush a rebellion for the Crown in 1215. For his services he was knighted and recognized as Earl of Ross in 1234.

The earldom of Ross in the north was ancient and its possessors held enormous power, judicial and otherwise. It was important to the southern-based monarchs that the earldom was held by suitable representatives and because of this, the title was awarded by successive kings to various holders.

A family of Ross acquired lands in Ayrshire and Renfrewshire in the twelfth century. They are believed to have come from Yorkshire, and a Godfrey de Ros obtained the lands of Stewarton in Cunningham.

Balnagown, Easter Ross, was the castle held by the ancient chiefly house of the Earls of Ross who

Rose Hunting

Ross Red Ancient

187

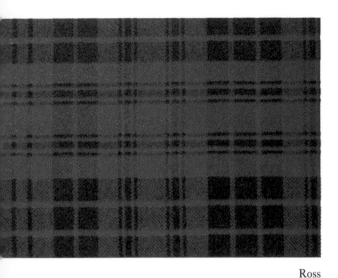

Ross

Ross Hunting

Rose Red Ancient

Russell

did not carry the surname of Ross – but when the title passed through the female line, they seem to have adopted the name as male representatives. In 1688, there were over forty Ross properties, but the lines dwindled and the chiefship has passed to the representatives of the Rosses of Shandwick.

Russell

A NAME ALLIED to the French Rosel. The Russells of Aden in Aberdeenshire descend from an English baron who accompanied Edward III of England at the siege of Berwick and decided to settle in Scotland. A Robert Russel of Berwickshire did forced homage to Edward I of England in 1296. Jerome Russell, a Greyfriars priest, was burned with John Kennedy for heresy in Glasgow in 1539.

Rutherford

THIS WAS ONCE a rich and powerful Border family who took the name from the lands of Rutherford in Maxton, Roxburghshire. The name appears in the reigns of William the Lion and Alexander II. A number of Rutherfords rendered forced homage to Edward I of England in 1296.

Daniel Rutherford, the discoverer of nitrogen, was born in Edinburgh in 1749.

Ruthven

FROM THE OLD BARONY of the name in Angus. Swan, son of Thor, son of Swein, held lands in Perthshire and Clydesdale and took the designation of de Ruthven. In 1488 Sir William Ruthven of that Ilk was created Lord Ruthven. His grandson, who married the heiress of the Haliburtons of Dirleton in East Lothian, was chosen Provost of Perth by royal command in 1528. Patrick Ruthven was one of the lords involved in the murder of David Rizzio, secretary to Mary, Queen of Scots. His son was rewarded for services to James VI by being created 1st Earl of Gowrie. In the Ruthven Raid he kidnapped the young king and held him prisoner for ten months. The king escaped and Gowrie was executed in 1584. The 2nd Earl of Gowrie inherited at the age of eleven. He was killed in Perth with his brother for supposedly attempting to kill the king in the Gowrie Conspiracy, but the information surrounding this event is highly suspect. The name of Gowrie was proscribed by law for forty years until the King of Sweden intervened to allow a Ruthven of Ballindean to use the name in 1639. The Act of Proscription was reversed in 1641.

Sir Thomas Ruthven was created Baron Ruthven of Freeland in 1651. Sir Alexander Hore-Ruthven of Freeland was Governor-General of Australia and was created Earl of Gowrie in 1945.

Ruthven

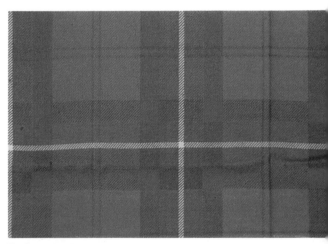

Ruthven Ancient

S(c)haw

THE LOWLAND SURNAME is of territorial origin, and is recorded in the thirteenth century. The southern families of this name are found mostly in Kircudbrightshire, Ayrshire and Stirlingshire.

The northern clan descends through Shaw, son of Gilchrist, grandson of the 6th Chief of Clan Mackintosh. He was granted lands in Rothiemurchus. The Shaws of Tordarroch, descendants of Adam, second son of

Schaw

189

Schaw of Tordarroch

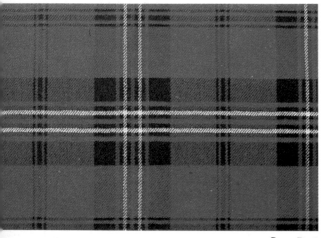

Scott Red

Rothiemurchus, now hold the Chiefship. They took protection from Clan Chattan.

Sir Thomas Shaw, Solicitor-General for Scotland (1894–5) and Lord Advocate (1905–9), was created Baron Craigmyle in 1929.

Scott

THIS IS a Border clan descended from Uchtredus filius Scoti, who lived in the twelfth century. His two sons were Richard, the ancestor of the Scotts of Buccleuch, and Sir Michael, the ancestor of the Scotts of Balweary.

The lordship of Scott of Buccleuch was created in 1606, and the earldom in 1619. Francis, 2nd Earl, had two daughters, successively Countesses of Buccleuch, the second of whom married James, Duke of Monmouth, natural son of Charles II. On their marriage in 1663 they were created Duke and Duchess of Buccleuch, each in their own right and, although Monmouth was subsequently beheaded and discredited for rebelling against his uncle, James VII and II, the Buccleuch title was passed to their eldest son by the Duchess. A later marriage linked the Buccleuchs with the powerful Douglas dukes of Queensberry.

Sir Michael Scott of Balweary was great-grandfather of another Sir Michael who was known as 'The Wizard'. The baronetcy became extinct (or dormant) on the death in 1902 of Sir William of Ancrum, 7th Baronet. Hugh Scott, 11th of Harden, succeeded to the lordship of Polwarth and Sir Walter Scott's family are connected with this line.

The Scotts were at their greatest as a Border clan in the sixteenth century. They could produce 600 men in a battle and they had their stronghold at Branxholm Castle, near Hawick. Through marriage, the Scotts of Buccleuch acquired Drumlanrig Castle, built in 1679 over a former Douglas stronghold. Dalkeith Palace and Bowhill, south-west of Selkirk, are owned by Buccleuch Estates. Bellenden, near the head of Ale Water, is the ancient gathering place of the Scotts.

Abbotsford House, west of Melrose, is the country house built by Sir Walter Scott; it almost brought him to bankruptcy before it was gifted to him by his creditors.

Scott Black and White

Scott Green

LEFT *Sir Walter Scott by Sir Henry Raeburn*
BELOW *Abbotsford House*

Sempill

THE SEMPILLS come from Elliotstoun in Renfrewshire and are the descendants of Robert de Semple (*c.* 1280), and they were hereditary Sheriffs of Renfrew. Sir John, 1st Lord Sempill, died at Flodden. The 4th Lord was James VI's Ambassador to Spain in 1596. Hugh, 12th Lord, fought for the Government at Culloden in 1745. The 15th Lord was succeeded by his sister, Maria Janet, who in turn was succeeded by her cousin, Sir William Forbes of Craigievar, a descendant of Patrick Forbes of Corse, armour bearer to James II. The family name was altered to Forbes-Sempill in consequence.

Craigievar Castle at Lumphanan is the Sempill seat and is owned by the National Trust for Scotland.

In Renfrewshire, at Lochwinnoch (part of the Clyde–Muirshiel Water Park), there are the ruins of Peel Castle, situated in the section known as Castle Semple Water Park. Also in ruins is Semple Collegiate Church, founded in 1504, and the Temple here is a folly built by a Lady Sempill.

Scrimgeour

Scrimgeour

Scrimgeour

THE NAME is recorded in the thirteenth century in connection with lands in Fife. Two documents issued in 1298 confirm lands on behalf of the Crown and Realm of Scotland by William Wallace and Robert Bruce. These confirm to Alexander Schyrmeschur, son of Colin, son of Carun, the perilous but honourable privilege of carrying the king's banner in war, the office of Constable of the Castle of Dundee, and certain lands in the Dundee neighbourhood. Later grants were made of lands near Inverkeithing, and lands were acquired through marriage to the heiress of Glassary.

John Scrymgeour was created Viscount Dudhope in 1641. John, 3rd Viscount, who was at the battle of Worcester in 1650, was created 1st Earl of Dundee in 1660.

Dudhope Castle, Dundee, was built by the Scrymgeours after Bannockburn to replace Dundee Castle. When the 1st Earl of Dundee died in 1668, he was succeeded by his kinsman John Scrymgeour of Kirkton, who was deprived of his lands through the influence of the 1st Duke of Lauderdale over Charles II. Dudhope Castle was later acquired by James Graham of Claverhouse, 1st Viscount Dundee, in 1683. Henry, 11th Earl, established his claim to the reinstatement of the title before the House of Lords in 1953.

Seton

WILLIAM THE LION gave a charter to Philip de Seton in 1169 of the lands of Seton, Winton and Winchburgh. Further lands were granted to Sir Alexander Seton by Robert Bruce in 1321.

The Setons played a significant role in Scottish affairs and became Lords Seton, Earls of Dunfermline and Earls of Winton. At the same time, they built many splendid residences for themselves: Seton Castle, rebuilt as Seton House by Robert Adam in 1790, where Mary, Queen of Scots fled after Rizzio's murder; Winton Castle, which said to have been built in 1480 by the 1st Lord Seton, but destroyed by the English in 1544, and rebuilt in 1619 by the 8th Lord Seton and 3rd Earl of Winton; and Pinkie House, Musselburgh, now incorporated in Loretto School. In the north

ABOVE *Seton House,
East Lothian*

RIGHT *Seton
Collegiate Church*

they purchased and rebuilt the magnificent Castle of Fyvie in Aberdeenshire.

James, 4th Earl of Dunfermline, through his family connection with the Gordons, brought out some of that clan to support Viscount Dundee's uprising and was outlawed and forfeited in 1690. George, 5th Earl of Winton, joined the Old Pretender in the 1715 uprising and was captured at the battle of Preston, attainted and forfeited, but escaped sentence of death by escaping from the Tower of London. James Seton, 3rd Viscount Kingston, and Sir George Seton of Garleton were also attainted and their titles forfeit.

The Setons of Abercorn acquired a Nova Scotia baronetcy in 1633, and the Setons of Pitmedden, also a Nova Scotia baronetcy, descend from a Lord of Justiciary, Lord Pitmedden; it was he who laid out the great garden of Pitmedden, now owned by the National Trust for Scotland.

Other Seton castles were Niddrie, south of Winchburgh, now ruined, to which Mary, Queen of Scots rode after her escape from Loch Leven, and Gogar Castle, on the outskirts of Edinburgh. Given by King Robert Bruce to Alexander Seton, the latter castle now has the National Trust for Scotland's Gardening Advice Centre (Suntrap) in the grounds.

Seton Collegiate Church in East Lothian has a fourteenth-century effigy of the 3rd Lord Seton, killed at the battle of Flodden.

Seton Hunting

Sinclair

SIR WILLIAM SAINT CLAIR, son of Robert de Saint Clair in Normandy, seemingly founded this clan. His son, Sir Henry de Sancto Claro, supported Robert Bruce and signed the letter to the Pope in 1320, asserting Scotland's independent rights.

St Clair of Rosslyn, a grandson, married a co-heiress of Malise, Earl of Strathearn, Caithness and Orkney. His eldest son obtained from King Hakon VI of Norway the right to the earldom of Orkney and received the earldom of Caithness in 1455. In 1470, the earldom of Orkney was

Sinclair Dress

OPPOSITE *Girnigoe Castle, formerly associated with the Sinclair family*

Sinclair Hunting

195

Roslin Castle

resigned to the Scottish Crown in exchange for Ravenscraig Castle, Kirkcaldy, which was finally demolished by General Monck in 1651.

Roslin Castle, Midlothian, is believed to have been founded by Sir William St Clair, although there is no substantial evidence. The keep was certainly expanded by William Sinclair, 3rd Earl of Orkney, who founded the nearby chapel in 1446. There is a story that Sir William St Clair wagered his head against the lands of Pentland that two of his hounds would pull down a deer before it reached a certain spot. The deer was killed just before it reached the given spot and Robert Bruce awarded the estate to St Clair. Roslin Castle today is a beautiful, if rather dilapidated, fortified house surrounded by the ruins of the former castle.

The Sinclairs held a number of castles in Caithness, notably at Noss Head, where they had Castle Sinclair in the fifteenth century and Girnigoe in the seventeenth century. The Castle of Mey, the Highland home of Queen Elizabeth, the Queen Mother, is a former Sinclair stronghold built by George, 5th Earl of Caithness, in 1568. Sir John Sinclair, the well-known agricultural improver (1754–1835), lived at Thurso Castle. Sir William Sinclair, founder and pastor of the first Baptist Church in Scotland, lived at Keiss Castle, which was built in the nineteenth century close to the former sixteenth-century tower.

196

Skene

IT IS SAID that the founder of this clan was offered by Malcolm Canmore as much land as was covered by a hawk's flight, and thus was formed the barony of Skene. The Skenes of Skene became extinct in the nineteenth century with the death of the last male descendant.

The lands of Skene and

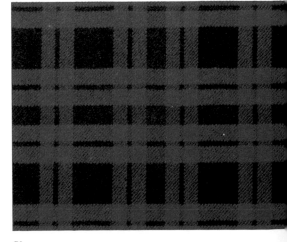

Skene

the part eighteenth-century Skene Castle are located in the Gordon district of Aberdeenshire. Skene's House in Aberdeen was built around 1545, but altered by Provost Skene of Aberdeen in the seventeenth century.

Somerville

THE NAME comes from a town near Caen in Normandy. William de Somerville came to Scotland with David I and was granted lands in Lanarkshire. A William de Somerville is believed to have killed a monstrous animal that was terrorizing the district of Linton in Roxburghshire during the reign of William the Lion and he was given the lands as a reward. Mary Somerville, a well-known scientific writer, lived at Burntisland in the 1780s.

Spalding

FROM THE TOWN of Spalding in Lincolnshire. The name is first recorded in Scotland in the thirteenth century. At the siege of Berwick in 1318 Peter de Spalding, a burgess of the town, decided to aid the besiegers. He was rewarded by Robert Bruce with lands in Angus together with the keepership of the Royal Forest of Kylgerry.

Spens

THE FAMILY is found in Scotland from the thirteenth century. Some contend that they descend from Duncan, 4th Earl of Fife, but there is no evidence to confirm this.

Patrick de Spens held lands in Lauder, Berwickshire, in the fifteenth century and John de Spensa of Perth had a grant of lands in Menteith. Thomas Spens was Bishop of Aberdeen in the fifteenth century.

Stewart, Stuart

THE ROYAL HOUSE OF STEWART, whose traditional descent was of old contrived to be from Banquo, Thane of Lochaber, has been historically traced to Alan, Seneschal of Dol, a Celtic noble. His nephew became Sheriff of Shropshire in England, and his third son, Walter Fitz Alan, became High Steward of Scotland in the reign of David I. He founded Paisley Abbey.

The office of High Steward was confirmed as an Hereditary Office by Malcolm IV. Walter's grand-

Stewart Royal

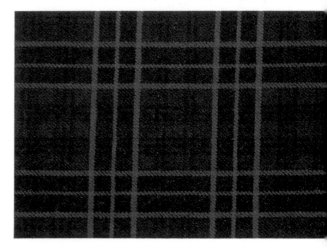

Stewart Old

197

Castle Stalker; see p. 202

son, Walter, was the first to adopt the title
'Steward' as a surname. Walter, 6th High
Steward, married Marjorie, daughter of King
Robert Bruce.

The origins of the Stewarts in Scotland are
essentially Lowland. They were the staunchest
upholders of national liberty. It should not be
forgotten that all that Bruce won for Scotland was
lost in the minority of his son, Scotland being once
again overrun by the English – and the prime
instrument of recovery and final establishment of
his country's freedom was gained by Bruce's
grandson, Robert Stewart, 7th Hereditary High
Constable of Scotland, later Robert II, first of the
Royal House of Stewart.

The Stewarts proved a remarkably prolific race
and had many offspring, legitimate and otherwise.
Sir John of Bonkyl (d. 1298) had seven sons –
among them Alexander, Earl of Angus, Alan, Earl
of Lennox, Walter, ancestor of the Earls of Galloway, and James, ancestor of the Earls of Buchan
and Traquair, as well as the Lords of Lorne and
Innermeath. Since the demise of the Lennox
branch, the Earls of Galloway have been regarded
as the senior representatives of the ancient line of
High Stewards of Scotland.

It can be appreciated then how the Stewarts
multiplied and spread through Scotland. In 1463,
for example, Sir John Stewart of Lorne was
murdered and his son, Dugald, sought to recover
the lordship from his uncle who had seized it. By
compromise he received the lands of Appin. Allan,
3rd of Appin, established the Appin clan by divid-
ing his lands between his five sons.

The Stewarts of Atholl descend from Sir John
Stewart of Balveny, half-brother of James II.
Dorothea, daughter of the 5th Earl, was wife of the
2nd Earl of Tullibardine, and so that earldom
passed into the Murray clan.

The Stuarts of Bute are descended from a
natural son of King Robert II. He was known as
the 'Black Stewart' to distinguish him from his
brother, John of Dundonald, nicknamed the 'Red
Stewart'.

Many of the Stewart kings came to violent ends.
James I was murdered at Perth in 1437; James II
was killed by a bursting cannon at the siege of
Roxburgh in 1460; James III died as he fled from
the battlefield of Sauchieburn in 1488; James IV
married Princess Margaret Tudor, daughter of
Henry VII of England, and was killed at Flodden in
1513 in battle against his brother-in-law, Henry
VIII of England; James V, who married Mary of

Stewart Hunting

Stewart of Athol

Stewart of Appin

ABOVE *Stirling Castle*

OPPOSITE *Doune Castle*

Guise, died in 1542, three weeks after the rout at Solway Moss.

Mary, James V's only daughter, was married to Dauphin Francis of France in 1558. He became King of France in 1559 and died in 1560. When Mary returned to her own realm, it was to a turbulent and divided land. Advised by her natural brother, whom she created Earl of Moray in 1561, her policies were successful and popular until her marriage to Lord Darnley, eldest son of the Earl of Lennox, and through Margaret Douglas, Countess of Lennox, a great-grandson of Henry VII of England. This marriage ensured that their son, James, became heir to the thrones of both England and Scotland. Darnley's murder in 1567 and Mary's marriage to the Earl of Bothwell led to her downfall and flight to England. She was executed in 1587 for alleged plotting against Queen Elizabeth I of England.

Mary's son, James VI, was an astute and devious ruler. Not for nothing was he known as the 'Wisest Fool in Christendom'. In 1603, he became King of England as James I and moved his court south to London. He died in 1625.

Charles I's policy of challenging Parliament and asserting his 'divine right' led ultimately to his execution at Whitehall in 1649, and a period of rule by the Commonwealth headed by Oliver Cromwell. The Scots, always loyal to the Stewarts,

agreed to bring Charles II from exile in Holland if he signed the Covenants. He was crowned at Scone in 1651, returned to exile, and was restored to the English throne in 1660 after Cromwell's death. He died in 1685, and his brother became James VII and II. His Catholic faith, however, was unacceptable to many, and when there was a revolution in support of his daughter, Mary, and her husband, William of Orange, both devout Protestants, James was forced to flee overseas.

William and Mary had no heir, and Mary's sister, Queen Anne, also died childless. In 1673, James VII and II had married Mary of Modena, a Catholic princess. Their son, James Francis, was by rights heir to the British throne, but his Catholicism was unacceptable to the Whig government of the day. They therefore approached a great-grandson of James VI and I, the Protestant George of Hanover, who became King of England and Scotland in 1714.

In 1715, James Francis, who became known as the 'Old Pretender', landed at Peterhead to join the Earl of Mar in an uprising against the usurping Hanoverians; but he departed soon after and spent the rest of his life in Rome, where he died in 1766. His eldest son, Prince Charles Edward, referred to by some as the 'Young Pretender' and 'Bonnie Prince Charlie', is the best known of the Stuarts, the 'Kings across the Water'. The uprising he led

Stewart Fingask

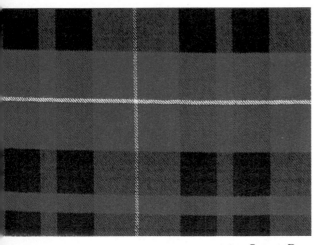

Stewart Bute

Stewart Bute Hunting

was ruthlessly crushed at Culloden Moor in 1745. The prince died in Rome in 1788, and was succeeded as *de jure* king by his brother, styled Henry IX, a Cardinal of the Church of Rome, who died without issue in 1807. The Jacobite claim to the thrones of Scotland and England has now passed to the Duke of Bavaria.

Note that the name of Stewart used by the Royal House was spelled Stuart after Mary, Queen of Scots' time in France.

The Royal Stewarts had their residences at Holyrood Palace in Edinburgh; at Linlithgow, birthplace of Mary, Queen of Scots; and Falkland in Fife, a favourite hunting lodge for James VI and I. Edinburgh Castle was the birthplace of James VI and I, and Stirling Castle was an important royal stronghold.

Doune Castle, overlooking the River Teith, was built towards the end of the fourteenth century by Robert Stewart, Regent of Scotland and Duke of Albany in the reign of Robert III. It is owned by the Earls of Moray. The Earls of Galloway had their seat at Galloway House, Garlieston. On the island of Bute, the Marquesses of Bute have their seat, Mount Stewart. Castle Stalker and Ardsheal House in Appin were owned by the Stewarts of Appin. Near Innerleithen in Peebles-shire is Traquair House, reputed to be the oldest inhabited house in Scotland. Sir John Stuart of Traquair was Lord High Treasurer of Scotland in the reign of Charles I. The Bear Gates in the grounds are 'never to be re-opened until a Stuart returns to the throne of Scotland'.

Stirling

THE NAME is taken from the town of that name, and the surname appears in the twelfth century. Sir John Stirling of Moray is recorded as having sworn fealty in 1291. A family of the name settled in the neighbourhood of Dunmaglass, Nairnshire.

The Stirlings of Keir on the outskirts of Stirling were established in the twelfth century.

Sir George Murray Home Stirling, CBE, DSO, 9th Nova Scotia Baronet, of Glorat, Stirlingshire, commanded the 9th Battalion Argyll and Sutherland Highlanders and was appointed Keeper of Dunbarton Castle by King George V in 1927.

Sutherland

THIS NAME originates in Sutherland, the 'Southland' of the Norsemen of Caithness and Orkney. The inhabitants of Sutherland are considered to descend from the Celts who retreated before the Norse invaders. The Chiefs originate from Freskin, progenitor of the Murrays. His youngest son, Hugh Freskin, received the lands of Sutherland from King William the Lion in 1197.

The earldom of Sutherland was created in the thirteenth century. Alexander, 11th Lord Strathnaver and Earl of Sutherland, died in 1594, and the male line continued until 1771, when the 17th Earl's daughter, Elizabeth, married George Granville Gower, 2nd Marquess of Stafford, who was created 1st Duke of Sutherland in 1833.

When the 5th Duke died, the chiefship and earldom of Sutherland passed to the daughter of the second son of the 4th Duke, and the dukedom passed to a grandson of the 2nd Duke.

The ancient castle of Dunrobin at Golspie has had the present Victorian structure built over it, and is the seat of the Earls of Sutherland. A statue of the 1st Duke of Sutherland can be seen near by on the top of Ben Braggie. He built the town of Golspie and was blamed for excessive Clearance evictions, which took almost the whole population of his lands overseas.

On the border of Ross and Cromarty and Easter Ross can be seen Carbisdale Castle, built by a Duchess of Sutherland and now a Youth Hostel.

Swinton

A FAMILY that held lands from David I near Duns in Berwickshire. They are thought to be of Anglian origin. Hugh of Swinton and his son Duncan acquired the thanedom of Arbuthnot from Walter Olifard and are thought to be the ancestors of the Arbuthnott family of Kincardineshire.

Henry de Swyntone of Berwickshire rendered forced homage to Edward I of England in 1296.

Stirling Dress

Sutherland Ancient

Sutherland

Morton Hall, Edinburgh

The name was carried to France in the fifteenth century and appears there as Vincton. The Swintons hold lands in Berwickshire to this day.

Trotter

THE NAME means literally 'messenger'. There was a Border clan of this name from Berwickshire, the head of which was Trotter of Prentannan. The Trotters of Morton Hall, Midlothian, are said to date back to the reign of Robert II (1370–90), and in the nineteenth century they have been a distinguished military family.

Turnbull

FOR SAVING THE LIFE of Robert Bruce when he was attacked by a wounded bull, one William of Rule was awarded lands and was thereafter known as Turne-e-bull. The Rule Water territory of the Turnbulls was a baronial possession of the House of Douglas. By 1510, the Turnbulls had become so scornful of the authority of James IV that he decided to make an example of them and 200 members of the family appeared before him wearing linen sheets, swords in hands and halters around their necks. Some were hanged and others imprisoned.

However, the unsettled state of the Borders continued, causing James VI and I to order his wardens to use 'hostile feud in hostile manner against all malefactors'. Many of the name of Turnbull left the Borders at this time. The chiefly branches of Bedrule and Minto fell into financial difficulties and scattered.

Turnbull castles were Barnshill, near the base of Minto Crags and built in the sixteenth century, and Bedrule, in the Rule Valley, which was destroyed by the English in 1545. They held Fulton Tower which is on the right of the Rule Water, and Minto estates on the River Teviot until these passed through various owners to the Elliots.

The Turnbulls owned Philiphaugh estates in the Ettrick Forest for 300 years. The Murrays acquired part of the lands through marriage, and then all of them after the last of the Turnbull line died in 1572.

Tweedie

AN OLD PEEBLES-SHIRE FAMILY said to have derived from a water spirit of the River Tweed. The name, however, would appear to derive from the lands of Tweedie in Lanarkshire.

Roger, son of Finlay of Twydyn, had a charter for the house and the lands of Drumelzier, near to Broughton. The family held the lands for 300 years and then had them confiscated in the reign of Charles I. The Tweedies were described as a domineering and powerful family, and a dispute with the Geddeses culminated with a James Geddes being murdered in Edinburgh.

Urquhart

Turnbull Dress

Turnbull Hunting

The Tweedies' stronghold at Drumelzier was called Tinnis Castle, but little now remains.

Urquhart

A SURNAME derived from the lands of Urquhart on Loch Ness. William Urquhart was Sheriff of Cromarty and married a daughter of the Earl of Ross in the fourteenth century.

Craigston Castle, 10 miles south-east of Banff, was the seat of the Urquhart family from 1604 to the present day. Their ancestral fortress was at Castle Craig, Udale Bay, on the Cromarty Firth. In 1449, a Thomas Urquhart was Bishop of Ross, and in 1585 the last Dean of Ross was an Urquhart. The Cromarty estate was sold to the Mackenzies, and the current chiefship of the clan is held by an American branch of the family.

Wallace

THE NAME Wallace means 'Strathclyde Briton' and is therefore considered a 'native' name. It was prominent in Ayrshire in the thirteenth century, and also in Renfrewshire. Richard Wallace (or Wallensis) or Richardston or Riccarton, who lived in the twelfth century, is the first noted of the name. He was in the  service of Walter Fitz Alan, first Steward of Scotland. His grandson, Adam, had two sons, Adam, 4th Laird of Riccarton in Ayrshire, and Malcolm, who received the lands of Elderslie and Auchinbothie in Renfrewshire. Malcolm was the father of Scotland's hero, Sir William Wallace (1274–1305) who led the revolt against English rule before his demise and the advent of victory achieved on the battlefield by Robert Bruce.

The Wallaces of Craigie, Ayrshire, are also descended from those of Riccarton.

At Stirling on the top of Abbey Craig stands the nation's memorial to William Wallace, built in 1896. Near Dryburgh Abbey in the Borders is a huge statue erected in his memory in 1814. There is also a statue at Lanark by sculptor Robert Forrest erected in 1882; this commemorates the tradition that it was the murder of Wallace's wife, who came from Lanark, that prompted him to take up arms against the English.

After several generations in Jamaica, a family of Wallace came forward as owners of the Busbie and Cloncaird estates in Ayrshire and were recognized as heads of the house of Wallace.

Wardlaw

WARDLAW, NEAR BEAULY, was kept by retainers of the Norman lord of the Aird, John Byset, in the early thirteenth century. But the Wardlaw family who probably took their name from this place are said to have been among the Anglo-Saxon families whose members fled to Scotland  at the time of the Norman Conquest to seek the protection of Malcolm Canmore.

Henricus de Wardlaw received a charter from Robert Bruce of half the barony of Wiltone in Roxburghshire. In the fifteenth century Henry Wardlaw, nephew of the Cardinal of that name, was Bishop of St Andrews who, apart from founding the University of St Andrews, was considered one of the most powerful and influential men of his time. From his brother, William, descend the Wardlaws of Pitreavie in Fife who acquired a Nova Scotia baronetcy in 1631.

Weir

A NAME of Norman origin from one of the places named Vere in France. The first of the name to be recorded in Scotland is one Radulphus de Ver, who was taken prisoner at Alnwick along with William the Lion.

The Weirs of Blackwood, Lanarkshire, claim descent from this gentleman, although they only appear on record in 1400, when they obtained their lands. Other Weirs appear as vassals of the Abbots of Kelso and held lands in Lesmahagow. Some of the Macnairs in

Wallace Hunting

The Wallace Monument, Stirling

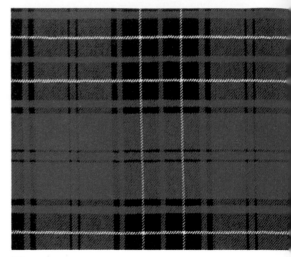

Weir   Wemyss

Cowal have anglicized their name to Weir. Major Thomas Weir of the Town Guard and his sister were burned for witchcraft in Edinburgh in 1670. In 1938 William Weir, born in Dumfries-shire, Chairman of the engineering company G. & J. Weir Ltd, Secretary of State and Chairman of the Air Council (1918), Industrial Adviser to the Ottawa Conference (1932), was created 1st Viscount Weir.

Wemyss

FROM THE LANDS of Wemyss in Fife. The first recorded of the name was Michael de Methkil, sometimes known as Michael de Wemys.

John Wemyss, created 1st Lord Wemyss of Elcho in 1628, and 1st Earl of Wemyss in 1633, eventually espoused the cause of the Covenant. David, 2nd Earl, constructed at his own cost the harbour of Methil in 1649. The 5th Earl was succeeded by his son, David, who was attainted in 1746, having supported Prince Charles Edward Stuart, and the Wemyss earldom passed to the Charteris of Amisfield family. The Wemyss estates and arms, however, devolved to the third son of the 5th Earl, as James Wemyss of Wemyss.

Wood

AS THE NAME derives from living near a wood, it is very widely spread throughout the country. Prominent families of the name settled in Morayshire and in the Borders, near Biggar in Lanarkshire. Sir Andrew Wood, from Largo in Fife, who died in 1515, was captain of the famous Scottish warship the *Yellow Carvel* and victor of a naval engagement in the Forth in 1498, when he both defeated and captured the English Admiral, Stephen Bull.

208

SEPT NAMES
AND ALLIED CLANS

NOTE   Many of the names of Scotland have been altered throughout the centuries since they were first written down, usually by the local clergy – who as often as not were the only persons able to do this. There was thus no standardization to begin with, and countless variations have developed. Different members of the same family are known to have taken protection from different clans and become followers of those clans. So in some cases you have brothers of the same family giving allegiance to different chiefs. Often names were simply territorial. The following is a simple guide, but it must be accepted that sometimes the same name is claimed by more than one clan. Obviously there are many names that have not been included and total accuracy cannot be guaranteed.

ABBOT MacNab
ABBOTSON MacNab
ADAM Gordon
ADAMSON Shaw and Mackintosh
ADIE Gordon
AIRLIE Ogilvy
ALAISTER MacDonald
ALCOCK MacDonald
ALEXANDER MacDonald and MacArthur
ALISON MacDonald
ALLAN MacDonald and MacFarlane
ALLANSON MacDonald and MacFarlane
ALLEN MacDonald
ALLISTER MacDonald
ALPIN MacAlpine
ANDERSON MacDonald and Ross
ANDREW Ross
ANGUS MacInnes
ARTHUR Campbell and MacArthur
AYSON Mackintosh
AYSON (NZ) Mackintosh and Shaw

BAIN Mackay and MacBain
BALLACH MacDonald
BALLOCH MacDonald
BANNATYNE Campbell
BANNERMAN Forbes
BAIN MacBain
BARTHOLOMEW Leslie and MacFarlane

BAXTER Macmillan
BAYN Mackay
BEAN MacBain
BEATH MacDonald
BEATON MacDonald, Macleod and Maclean
BELL Macmillan
BETHUNE MacDonald
BLACK Maclean, Lamont and MacGregor
BOWIE MacDonald
BRIEVE Morrison
BRODIE MacDonald
BROWN Lamont
BUCHAN Comyn
BUDGE MacDonald
BUIE MacDonald
BULLOCH MacDonald
BURNS Campbell
BURNESS Campbell
BURNETT Campbell

CADEL Campbell
CADDELL Campbell
CAIRD Sinclair and MacGregor
CALDER Campbell
CALLAN MacDonald
CALLEN MacDonald
CAMBRIDGE MacDonald
CARMICHAEL MacDougall
CARRISTON Skene
CASKIE Macleod
CATHAL MacDonald
CATHIL MacDonald
CATTANACH Macpherson

CATTELL Campbell
CHALMERS Campbell
CHARLSON Mackenzie
CHEYNE Sutherland
CLARK Macpherson and Mackintosh
CLARKE Macpherson and Mackintosh
CLERK Macpherson and Mackintosh
CLERKSON Macpherson and Cameron
CLOUSTON Sinclair
COCHRAN MacDonald
COCHRANE MacDonald
COLL MacDonald
COLLYEAR Donnachaidh
COLMAN Buchanan
COLSON MacDonald
COMB MacThomas
COMBIE MacThomas
COMMYN Comyn
CONN MacDonald
CONNACHER MacDonald
CONNAL MacDonald
CONNEL MacDonald
CONNOCHIE Campbell
COOK MacDonald
COOKE MacDonald
COULSON MacDonald
COUTTS Farquharson
COWAN MacDonald and Colquhoun
CRAWFORD Lindsay
CRERAR Mackintosh
CROMB MacDonald

CROMBIE MacDonald and Gordon
CROOM MacDonald
CRUM MacDonald
CURRIE MacDonald and Macpherson

DALLAS Mackintosh
DANIEL MacDonald
DANIELS MacDonald
DARRACH MacDonald
DARROCH MacDonald
DAVIE Davidson and Clan Chattan
DAVIS Davidson and Clan Chattan
DAWSON Davidson and Clan Chattan
DENOON Campbell
DEUCHAR Lindsay
DEWAR MacNab
DINGWALL Ross and Munro
DIS Skene
DOCHART MacGregor
DONACHIE Donnachaidh
DONALD MacDonald
DONALDSON MacDonald
DONLEAVY Buchanan
DONNELL MacDonald
DONNELSON MacDonald
DONNILSON MacDonald
DONNOCHY Donnachaidh

DOUGAL MacDougal
DOW Davidson and Clan Chattan
DRAIN MacDonald
DUFFIE MacFie
DUFFY MacFie
DUNCAN Donnachaidh
DUNCANSON Donnachaidh
DUNNACHIE Donnachaidh
DUNNEL MacDonald
DUNSMORE Murray
DUNURE Campbell
DYCE Skene

EANRIG Gunn
EDIE Gordon
ELDER Mackintosh
ENNIS Innes
ENRICH Gunn
ESSON Shaw and Mackintosh
EWAN MacLachlan
EWEN MacLachlan
EWING MacLachlan

FAIL MacPhail
FALL MacPhail
FARQUHAR Farquharson
FEDERETH Sutherland
FERGUS Fergusson
FERRIES Fergusson
FERSON Macpherson
FINDLAY Farquharson
FINDLAYSON Farquharson
FLEMING Murray
FLETCHER MacGregor
FORDYCE Forbes
FORREST MacDonald
FOULIS Munro

GAIRE Gair
GAINSON Gunn and Sinclair
GALLIE Gunn
GALBRAITH MacDonald
GALBREATH MacDonald
GALL MacDonald
GALT MacDonald
GAUL MacDonald
GAULD MacDonald
GAYER Gair
GAYRE Gair
GEARE Gair
GEERE Gair
GEORGESON Gunn
GIBB Buchanan
GIBBON Campbell

GIBSON Buchanan and Campbell
GILBERTSON Buchanan
GILBRIDGE MacDonald
GILCHRIST Ogilvy
GILFILLAN MacNab
GILL MacDonald
GILLANDERS Ross
GILLESPIE Macpherson
GILLON Macpherson
GILMORE Morrison
GILROY Grant
GLEN Mackintosh
GLENNIE Mackintosh
GOLLAN Mackintosh
GORRIE MacDonald
GORRY MacDonald
GOW Macpherson
GOWAN MacDonald
GOWANS MacDonald
GRAY Sutherland
GREGOR MacGregor
GREGORSON MacGregor
GREGORY MacGregor
GREIG MacGregor
GREVSACK Fergusson
GRIER MacGregor
GRIGOR MacGregor
GRIMMOND Macleod
GRUER MacGregor

HALLYARD Skene
HANNA Hannay
HANNAH Hannay
HARDIE Fergusson and Mackintosh
HARDY Fergusson and Mackintosh
HARPER Buchanan
HARPERSON Buchanan
HARRES Campbell
HARRIS Campbell
HASTINGS Campbell
HAWES Campbell
HAWSON Campbell
HAWTHORN MacDonald
HEGGIE Mackintosh
HENDERSON Gunn and MacDonald
HENDRIE MacDonald
HENDRY MacNaughton and MacDonald
HENRY MacDonald
HERON MacDonald
HEWISON MacDonald
HOUSTON MacDonald
HOWAT MacDonald
HOWE MacDonald
HOWIE MacDonald
HOWISON MacDonald

HUDSON MacDonald
HUGHSON MacDonald
HUNTLY Gordon
HUTCHEON MacDonald
HUTCHESON MacDonald
HUTCHIN MacDonald
HUTCHISON MacDonald
HUTCHON MacDonald
HUTSON MacDonald

INCHES Donnachaidh
INNIS Innes
ISAAC MacDonald and Campbell
ISAACS MacDonald and Campbell
ISLES MacDonald
IVERSON Campbell

JAMIESON Gunn
JEFFREY MacDonald
JOHNSON MacDonald and Gunn
JOHNSTONE MacDonald

KAY Davidson and Clan Chattan
KEAN MacDonald and Gunn
KEEGAN MacDonald
KEENE MacDonald
KEITH Sutherland
KELLAR Campbell
KELLER Campbell
KELLY MacDonald
KENDRICK MacNaughton
KENNETH Mackay
KENNETHSON Mackay
KETCHEN MacDonald
KILPATRICK Colquhoun
KINNEL MacDonald
KIRKPATRICK Colquhoun
KISSACK Campbell
KISSOCK Campbell

LACHLAN MacLachlan
LANG Gair, Leslie and Donnachaidh
LAING Gair and Donnachaidh
LAMB Lamont
LAMBIE Lamont
LAMONDSON Lamont
LANDERS Lamont
LEAN Maclean
LECHY MacGregor
LECKIE MacGregor

LECKY MacGregor
LEES Macpherson
LEITCH MacDonald
LENNY Buchanan
LEYS Farquharson
LINKLATER Sinclair
LOBBAN Logan
LORNE Campbell
LOUDON Campbell
LOVE Mackintosh
LOWDON Campbell
LUCAS Lamont
LUKE Lamont
LYON Farquharson

MACACHIN MacDonald
MACADIE Fergusson
MACAICHAN MacDonald
MACALDINE Lamont
MACALDONICH Buchanan
MACALLAN MacDonald
MACANDEOIR Buchanan
MACANDEOIR MacNab
MACANDREW Mackintosh and Ross
MACANGUS Innes
MACARA Gregor and MacRae
MACARTAIR Campbell and MacDonald
MACARTER MacArthur
MACARTHUR Campbell and MacDonald
MACAULAY Macleod
MACAUSELAN Buchanan
MACAUSLEN Buchanan
MACAY Shaw and Mackintosh
MACBAXTER Macleod
MACBEATH MacBain, MacDonald and Maclean
MACBETH MacBain and Maclean
MACBHEATH MacDonald
MACBRAYNE MacDonald and MacNaughton
MACBRIDE MacDonald
MACBRIEVE Morrison
MACBRYDE MacDonald
MACBURIE MacDonald
MACCAA MacDonald
MACCAIG Farquharson and Macleod
MACCAINSH Innes
MACCAIRN MacDonald

MacCALMAN Buchanan
MacCALMONT Buchanan
MacCALLUM Macleod
MacCAMBRIDGE MacDonald
MacCARDNEY Farquharson and Mackintosh
MacCARRON MacDonald
MacCARTER Campbell
MacCAW MacDonald
MacCAY MacDonald
MacCEOL MacNaughton
MacCHLERIC Cameron and Macpherson
MacCHLERY Campbell, Mackintosh and Macpherson
MacCHOITER MacGregor
MacCHRUITER Buchanan
MacCLERIE Mackintosh
MacCLERISH Mackintosh
MacCLERY Cameron
MacCLUSKIE MacDonald
MacCLYMONT Lamont
MacCOLM MacThomas
MacCOMAS MacThomas
MacCOMBIE MacThomas
MacCOMIE MacThomas
MacCOMISH MacThomas
MacCONNACHER Macdougall
MacCONNAL MacDonald
MacCONNECHY Campbell
MacCONNELL MacDonald
MacCONNELLY Mackintosh
MacCONNOCHIE Campbell
MacCORKILL Gunn
MacCORMACK Buchanan
MacCORMICK MacLaine of Lochbuie
MacCOSHAM MacDonald
MacCOWAN Colquhoun, MacDonald and Macdougall
MacCOY Mackay
MacCULLOCH Macdougall, Munro and Ross
MacCUNN Macqueen
MacCURIE MacDonald
MacCURRACH MacDonald
MacCURRACK Macpherson
MacCUTCHEN MacDonald
MacCUTCHEON MacDonald
MacDADE Davidson
MacDAID Davidson
MacDAVID Davidson
MacDERMID Campbell
MacDERMOTT Campbell
MacDIARMID Campbell
MacDONNACHIE Donnachaidh
MacDOWELL MacDougall
MacELLER Campbell
MacELVER Campbell
MacELVIE Campbell
MacERACHER Farquharson
MacEVER Campbell
MacEWAN MacLachlan
MacEWEN MacLachlan
MacFADYEN MacLaine of Lochbuie
MacFADZEAN MacLaine of Lochbuie
MacFAIL MacPhail
MacFARQUHAR Farquharson
MacFAUL MacPhail
MacFERGUS Fergusson
MacGERUSICK Buchanan
MacGIBBON Buchanan and Campbell
MacGILBERT Buchanan
MacGILCHRIST Ogilvy and MacLachlan
MacGILLEDOW Lamont
MacGILLIVOOR MacGillivray
MacGILLONE Cameron
MacGILROY Grant and MacGillivray
MacGILVRA MacLaine of Lochbuie
MacGILVRAY MacGillivray
MacGLASRICH Campbell
MacGOUGHAN MacDougall
MacGOWAN Gow and Macpherson
MacGROUTHER MacGregor
MacGROWTHER Drummond
MacGRORY Maclaren
MacGRUDER Drummond and MacGregor
MacGRUTHER MacGregor
MacGRUITTE MacGregor
MacGUBBIN Campbell
MacGUFFIE MacFie
MacGURE Campbell
MacHARDIE Mackintosh
MacHARDY Mackintosh
MacHAY Shaw
MacHENDRY MacNaughton
MacIAN Gunn
MacIARRAN Grant
MacILDOWIE Campbell
MacILROY Grant
MacILVIAN MacBain
MacILVORA MacLaine of Lochbuie
MacINALLY Buchanan
MacINDEOIR Buchanan
MacINDOE Buchanan
MacINLAY Fergusson
MacINNES Innes
MacINROY Donnachaidh
MacISAAC Campbell and MacDonald
MacIVER Campbell and Donnachaidh
MacIVOR Campbell, Mackenzie and Donnachaidh
MacJAMES MacFarlane
MacKAFFIE MacFie
MacKAIMES Gunn
MacKAIL Cameron
MacKEAMISH Gunn
MacKEE Mackay
MacKEGGIE Mackintosh
MacKEITH Macpherson
MacKELLAR Campbell
MacKELVIE Campbell
MacKENDRICK MacNaughton
MacKENRACH MacNaughton
MacKERLICH Mackenzie
MacKERLIE Campbell
MacKERRACHER Farquharson
MacKERRAN Grant
MacKERRAS Fergusson
MacKERSEY Fergusson
MacKESSACK Campbell
MacKESSOCK Campbell
MacKEY Mackintosh
MacKICHAN MacDougall
MacKIE Mackay
MacKINLAY MacFarlane and Buchanan
MacKINNEY Mackinnon
MacKINNY Mackinnon
MacKINVEN Mackinnon
MacKISSOCK Campbell
MacKNIGHT MacNaughton
MacLAGGAN Donnachaidh
MacLaws Campbell
MacLEHOSE Campbell
MacLEISH Macpherson
MacLEISTER MacGregor
MacLENNY Maclean
MacLERIE Macpherson
MacLISE Macpherson
MacLIVER MacGregor
MacLOOCH MacFarlane
MacLUGASH MacDougall
MacLUKAS MacDougall and Lamont
MacLULICH MacDougall, Munro and Ross
MacLURE Macleod
MacMARTIN Cameron
MacMASTER Buchanan
MacMATH Matheson
MacMATHIE Matheson
MacMAURICE Buchanan
MacMORRAN Mackinnon
MacMURCHIE Buchanan and Mackenzie
MacMURDO Macpherson

MacMurdoch Macpherson
MacMurich Macpherson
MacMurray Murray
MacNair MacFarlane and MacNaughton
MacNayer MacNaughton
MacNee MacGregor
MacNei MacGregor
MacNeilage MacNeil
MacNeish MacGregor
MacNelly MacNeil
MacNichol Campbell
MacNemell MacDougall
MacNides MacFarlane
MacNish MacGregor
MacNiter MacFarlane
MacNiven Comyn, Mackintosh and MacNaughton
MacNocaird Campbell
MacNuyer Buchanan
MacOmish MacThomas
MacOnachie Campbell
MacOnie Campbell
MacOran Campbell
MacOwen Campbell
MacPatrick Lamont and MacLaren
MacPaul MacPhail
MacPeter MacGregor
MacPetrie MacGregor
MacPhadden MacLaine of Lochbuie
MacPhail Mackay
MacPhal MacPhail
MacPhaul MacPhail
MacPhedran Campbell and MacAulay
MacPhedron MacAulay
MacPhun Campbell
MacQuattie Forbes
MacQuey Mackay
MacQuoid Mackay
Macra MacRae
MacRaith MacRae
MacRankin Maclean
MacRath MacRae
MacRitchie Mackintosh

MacRob Gunn and Innes
MacRobbie Gair, Donnachaidh and Drummond
MacRobert Donnachaidh
MacRoy Maclaren
MacSorly Cameron and Lamont
MacSwan Macqueen
MacSween Macqueen
MacSwen Macqueen
MacSwyle Macqueen
MacTaggart Ross
MacTary Innes
McTavish Campbell
MacTear Mackintyre and Ross
MacThearlaich - Mackenzie
MacUalrig Cameron
MacUlric Cameron
MacUre Campbell
MacVail Mackay
MacVanish Mackenzie
MacVeag Maclean
MacVean MacBain
MacVey Maclean
MacVinish Mackenzie
MacVicar MacNaughton
MacWalter MacFarlane
MacWatt Forbes
MacWattie Buchanan
MacWhirter Buchanan
MacWilliam Gunn and MacFarlane
Manson Gunn
Marioch Innes
Martin Cameron of Erracht
Martyne Cameron of Erracht
Masterson Buchanan
Mathie Matheson
Mauchlan MacLachlan
Mavor Innes
Meikleham Lamont
Middleton Innes
Milne Gordon and Ogilvy
Mitchell Innes

Moore Campbell
Moray Murray
More Leslie
Mowat Sutherland
Muir Campbell
Murchie Mackenzie
Murchison Mackenzie
Murdoch Macpherson
Murdoson Macpherson

Neal MacNeil
Neil MacNeil
Neill MacNeil
Neilson Mackay
Nelson Gunn
Nicol Macleod
Nicolson Macleod
Niven Comyn, MacNaughton and Mackintosh
Noble Mackintosh
Norman Macleod
Norrie Skene
Norris Gair

Ochiltree Campbell
Oliphant Sutherland
Orr Campbell
Oynie Innes

Parker Gair
Patrick Lamont
Patten Maclaren
Patterson Maclaren
Paul Cameron, Mackintosh and Mackay
Pinkerton Campbell
Polson Mackay
Pyper Murray

Rankin Maclean
Ray Donnachaidh
Reach Farquharson
Reid Donnachaidh
Reidford Innes
Ritchie Mackintosh
Riach Farquharson
Risk Buchanan
Robson Gunn
Ruskin Buchanan
Russell Comyn

Sandison Gunn
Scaith Shaw
Seath Mackintosh

Seith Shaw
Shaith Shaw
Shaw Mackintosh
Shay Shaw
Sheach Shaw
Sheath Shaw
Shiach Shaw
Smail Murray
Small Murray
Smeal Murray
Sorley Cameron and Lamont
Spalding Murray
Spittal Buchanan
Spittel Buchanan
Stark Donnachaidh
Swan Macqueen
Swanson Gunn

Taggart Ross
Tarril Mackintosh
Tawesson Campbell
Tawson Campbell
Taylor Cameron
Thane Innes
Thom MacThomas
Thomas MacThomas
Thoms MacThomas
Thompson Campbell
Thomson MacThomas
Todd Gordon
Tolmie Macleod
Torrie Campbell
Torry Campbell
Tosh Mackintosh
Toshech Mackintosh
Toward Lamont
Towart Lamont
Train MacDonald
Turner Lamont
Tyre MacIntyre

Ure Campbell

Wass Ross and Munro
Weaver MacFarlane
Weir MacFarlane
Wheelan MacDonald
Whellan MacDonald
Whennel MacDonald
White Lamont and MacGregor
Whyte MacGregor
Wilkie MacDonald
Wilkison MacDonald
Wilson Innes

Yunie Innes

THE MATRICULATED STANDARDS
OF THE CLAN CHIEFS

These drawings were prepared for use during the International Gathering of the Clans which took place in Scotland in 1977. At that time many of the Clan Chiefs or Heads of Families had not matriculated their personal Standards with the Lyon Court. Since then, however, the following Standards have been officially matriculated (although we regret that it has not been possible to reproduce them with these original drawings): Anstruther, Bruce, Cameron, Carmichael, Cranston, Forsyth, Hannay, Hunter, Jardine, Johnstone, Lennox, Lumsden, Mackenzie, MacLennan, Macmillan, Maitland, Nicholson, Scrymgeour and Wedderburn.

Note that there are Standards illustrated for both Erskine and Mar. These relate to the *two* earldoms of Mar: *see* the entry for Erskine, p. 89.

A standard is used to mark the location of a chief's headquarters and rallying point for his Clansman. Each is the personal property of its owner, the Chief of a Scottish Clan. They are protected by the laws in Scotland and none may be flown without the consent of its owner, the Chief. In the 'hoist', nearest the pole they show either the national Scottish saltire or the personal arms of the Chief. The rest of the standard is made up of the Chief's livery colours, and shows his Crest (which is also the centre of the Clansman's bonnet badge) with or without his other heraldic or plant badges used by the Clan but vested in the Chief of the Clan. His motto or slogan is shown on the transverse bands.

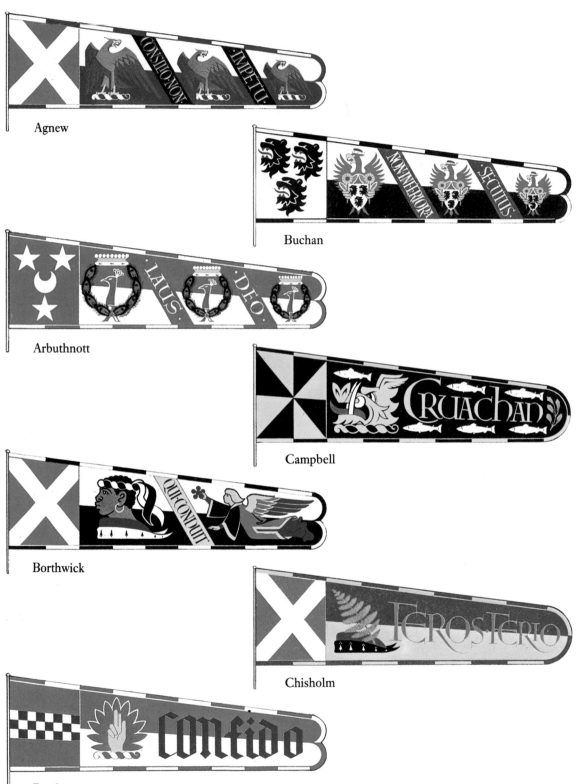

Agnew

Buchan

Arbuthnott

Campbell

Borthwick

Chisholm

Boyd

Clan Chattan

Eliott

Colquhoun

Erskine

Drummond

Farquharson

Dunbar

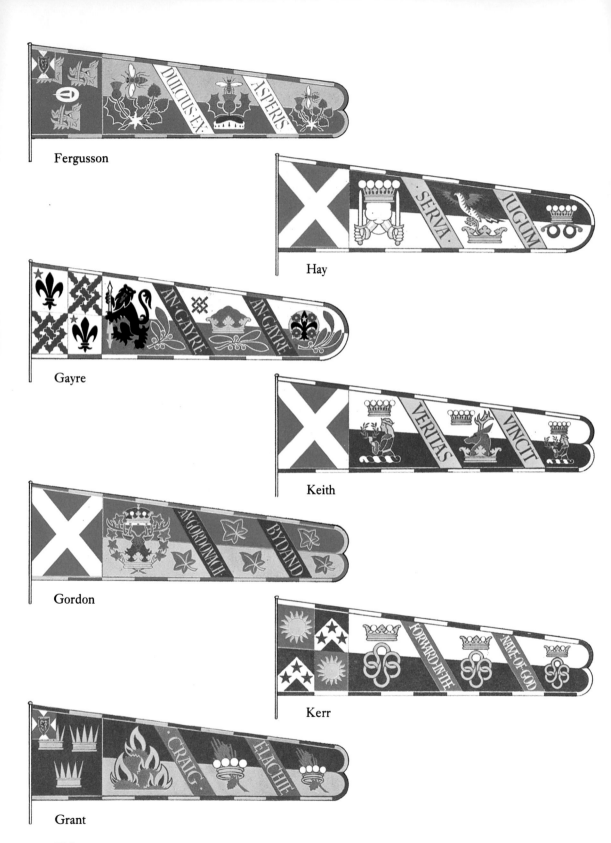

Fergusson

Hay

Gayre

Keith

Gordon

Kerr

Grant

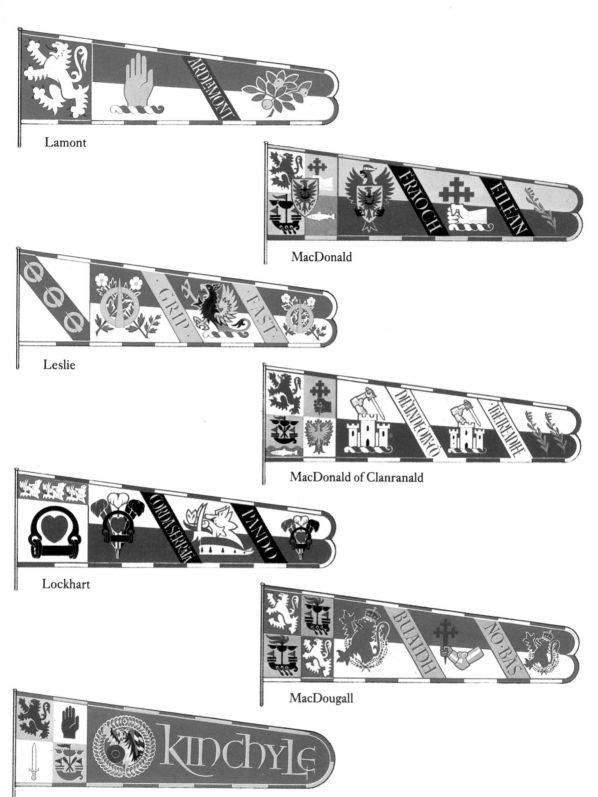

Lamont

MacDonald

Leslie

MacDonald of Clanranald

Lockhart

MacDougall

MacBain

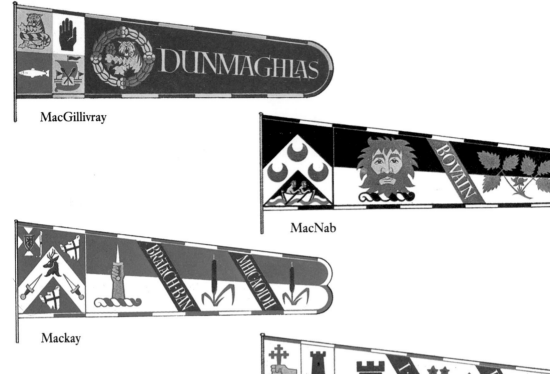

MacGillivray

MacNab

Mackay

MacNaughton

Mackintosh

MacNeil

Maclaren

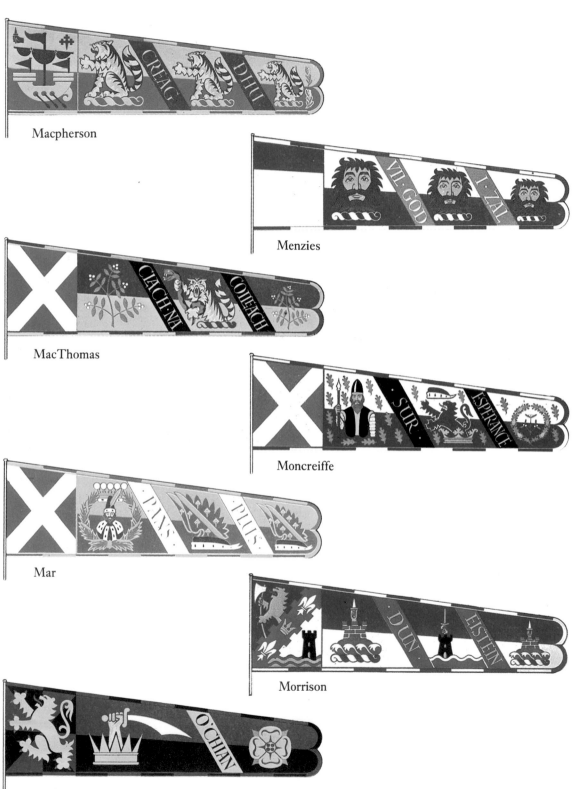

Macpherson

Menzies

MacThomas

Moncreiffe

Mar

Morrison

Matheson

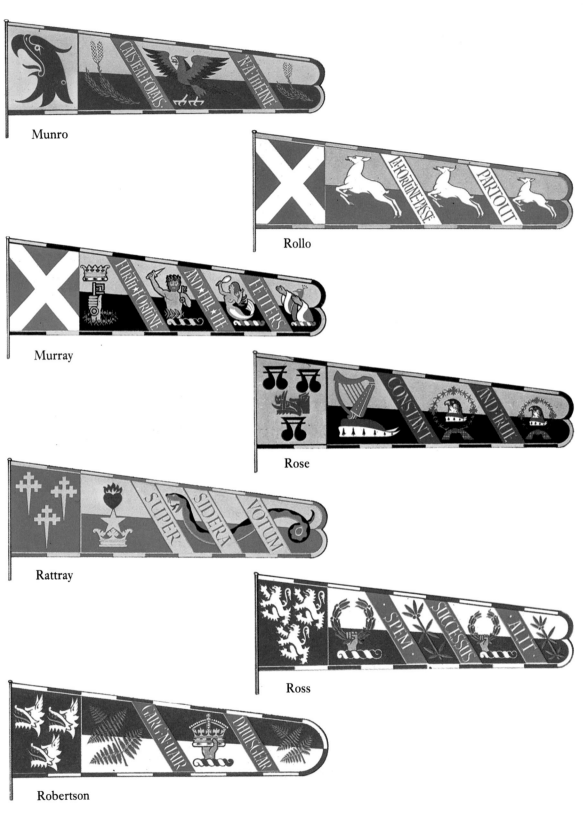

Munro

Rollo

Murray

Rose

Rattray

Ross

Robertson

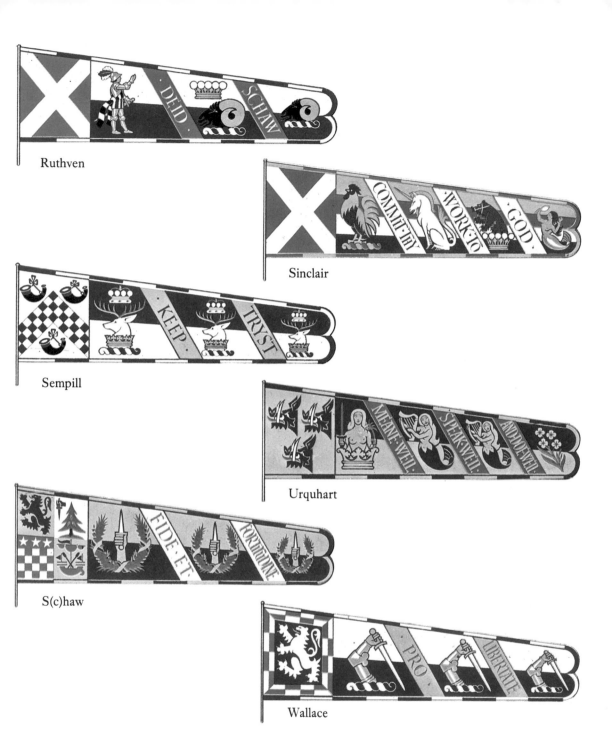

Ruthven

Sinclair

Sempill

Urquhart

S(c)haw

Wallace

GLOSSARY

of some Genealogical and Clan terms

ARD RIGH The High King. The Ard Righ was superior to the Righ or provincial kings.

BROKEN MEN Clan followers without specific family allegiance who gave their allegiance in return for protection.

CEANN MOR or CANMORE Gaelic for 'big head'.

CEANCATH War leader.

CHIEFTAIN Head of a minor or secondary branch of a clan owing allegiance to a chief.

CLAYMORE Scottish broadsword.

COCKADE A plume, usually of feathers, worn in a bonnet.

DISTRICT TARTAN A pattern associated with a certain area of the country, but not necessarily having any clan significance.

DUTHUS Headquarters.

EAGLE'S FEATHERS A clan chief wears three in his bonnet; a chieftain has two.

GARDE ÉCOSSAIS The Scottish Archer Guard of the King of France, founded 1455.

GILFINE A council consisting of nine members representing a clan.

HIGHLAND CLEARANCES The process by which the Highland crofting community was dispersed throughout the eighteenth and nineteenth centuries to make way for sheep farming.

LORD LYON KING OF ARMS The High Sennachie of Scotland presiding over lineage and heraldic matters. In Scotland, Lyon represents 'part of the very presence of the Sovereign'.
Lyon Court The body that recognizes heraldic and titular claims. All recognized tartans are registered with Lyon Office.

MATRICULATE To receive official recognition from Lyon.

MORMAER An early ruler of a Scottish province, a title that predated the great Highland earldoms of Scotland.

OF THAT ILK Senior representative of the name.

PLAD or PLAID The original blanket-style dress of the Highlander of tartan design which gave way to the kilt as we know it today.

SALTIRE A white St Andrew's cross on a blue background; the symbol and flag of Scotland.

SEPT A name associated with a particular clan.

SGIAN DUBH A knife carried in the sock when wearing modern Highland dress. Although long ago it undoubtedly had a practical use, it is nowadays simply a decorative accessory.

'VESTIARIUM SCOTICUM' The book published by the Sobieski Stuart brothers to authenticate tartan and which proved to be a monumental hoax.

PHILABEG The little kilt or half kilt, as worn today.

PROSCRIPTION, Act of (1746) Parliamentary legislation by which the wearing of tartan was prohibited.

BIBLIOGRAPHY

ADAM, F. *The Clans, Septs and Regiments of the Scottish Highlands.* 1908

BAIN, R. *The Clans and Tartans of Scotland.* 1938

BARROW, G. V. S. *Robert Bruce.* 1965

—— *The Anglo-Norman Era in Scottish History.* 1980

BLACK, G. F. *The Surnames of Scotland: Their Origin, Meaning and History.* 1946

BUCHAN, J. *The Marquis of Montrose.* 1913

—— *Montrose.* 1928

BULLOCH, J. M. *The House of Gordon.* 1903

BURN, M. *The Debatable Land.* 1970

CHAMBERS, R. *History of the Rebellions of Scotland under the Marquis of Montrose.* 1928

CROMARTIE, Earl of. *A Highland History.* 1980

DAICHES, D. *A Companion Guide to Scottish Culture.* 1981

DUNBAR, J. T. *History of Highland Dress.* 1962

FENWICK, R. *Scotland's Castles.* 1976

FRASER, Lady Antonia. *Mary Queen of Scots.* 1969

FRASER, Sir W. *The Montgomeries, Earls of Eglinton,* 2 vols. 1859

—— *The Maxwells of Pollok,* 2 vols. 1863.

—— *The Maxwells, Herries and Nithsdale Muniments.* 1865

—— *History of the Carnegies, Earls of Southesk,* 2 vols. 1869

—— *The Lennox,* 2 vols. 1874

—— *The Earls of Cromartie,* 2 vols. 1876

—— *The Scotts of Buccleuch,* 2 vols. 1876

—— *The Frasers of Philorth,* 3 vols. 1879

—— *The Chiefs of Grant,* 3 vols. 1883

—— *The Douglas Book,* 4 vols. 1885

—— *The Family of Wemyss,* 3 vols. 1888

—— *The Earls of Haddington,* 2 vols. 1889

—— *The Melvilles, Earls of Melville, and the Leslies, Earls of Leven,* 3 vols. 1890

—— *The Sutherland Book,* 3 vols. 1892

—— *The Earls of Annandale,* 2 vols. 1894

—— *Lords Elphinstone, Balmerino and Coupar,* 2 vols. 1897

GLADSTONE, I. O. J. *The Lauries of Maxwelton and Other Laurie Families.* 1972

GRANGE, R. M. D. *A Short History of Scottish Dress.* 1966

GRANT, I. F. *The Macleods: The History of the Clan 1200–1956.* 1959

HESKETH, C. *Tartans.* 1961

INNES OF LEARNEY, Sir T. *The Tartans of the Clans and Families of Scotland.* 1938

LINDSAY, Lord. *The Lives of the Lindsays.* 1858

MACDONALD OF CASTLETON, D. J. *Clan Donald.*

MCIAN, R. R., and LOGAN, J. *The Clans of the Scottish Highlands.* 1845

MACKENZIE, W. C. *The Life and Times of the Earls of Southesk,* 2 vols. 1867

MCKIE, R. L. *A Short History of Scotland.* 1930

MACKINNON, D. *The Macleods: The Genealogy of the Clan.* 1976

MACKINTOSH OF MACKINTOSH, M. *The Clan Mackintosh and the Clan Chattan.* 1948

MACLAREN OF MACLAREN, M. *The MacLarens.* 1960

MACMILLAN, S. *The MacMillans and Their Septs.* 1952

MCNITT, V. V. *The MacNaughton Saga.* 1951

MARTINE, R. *Homelands of the Scots.* 1981

—— *Clans and Tartans.* 1982

MITCHISON, R. *A History of Scotland.* 1970

MONCREIFFE OF THAT ILK, Sir I. *The Highland Clans.* 1982

MUNRO, R. W. *Highland Clans and Tartans.* 1977

—— *Scotland: Land of Kin and Clan.* 1980

MUNRO, R. W. and J. *The Scrimgeours.* 1980

ROSS, J. R. *The Great Clan Ross.* 1972

SCARLETT, J. D. *Scotland's Clans and Tartans.* 1974

—— *The Tartans of the Scottish Clans.* 1975

SHAW OF TORDARROCH, Major C. J. *A History of the Clan Shaw.* 1983

SIMPSON, W. D. *Scottish Castles.* 1959

SKENE, W. F. *A History of the Highland Clans.* 1837

SMOUT, T. C. *History of the Scottish Peoples.*

STEWART, D. C. *The Setts of the Scottish Tartans.* 1950

STEWART, D. C., and Thomson, J. C. *Scotland's Forged Tartans: An Analytical Study of the Vestiarium Scoticum.*

STRATHSPEY, Lord. *A History of Clan Grant.* 1983

TAYLER, A. and H. *The House of Forbes.* 1937

—— *The Book of the Duffs.*

WILLIAMS, R. *Montrose: Cavalier in Mourning.* 1975

INDEX OF CASTLES AND HOUSES

Numbers in *italics* refer to illustrations